Confederation on the March

Confederation on the March

VIEWS ON MAJOR CANADIAN
ISSUES DURING THE SIXTIES

THE RIGHT HONOURABLE
VINCENT MASSEY, C.H.

Macmillan of Canada
TORONTO
1965

Acknowledgment is made to the original publishers of two of the addresses in this volume: the Oxford University Press for 'Canadians and Their Commonwealth', and the Queen's Printer, Ottawa, for 'To Meet the Commonwealth'. 'An Introduction to Canada' first appeared in *Conference across a Continent*, published by The Macmillan Company of Canada Limited.

Printed in Canada for The Macmillan Company of Canada Limited, 70 Bond Street, Toronto, by the T. H. Best Printing Company Limited.

Contents

Confederation on the March

Confederation
on the March

*An address given at the Biennial Conference of the Association
of Canadian Clubs, in Charlottetown,
June 1, 1964.*

I AM VERY GLAD to be back in Prince Edward Island. I think I should probably have said '*the* Island'. I have heard this charming province called 'the Island' thousands of miles from Charlottetown, even on the West Coast not far from Vancouver Island, and no one seemed to mind.

Puisque les Clubs Canadiens font parti d'un mouvement national, ils exigent la collaboration des citoyens de langues française et anglaise tels qu'on trouve dans les Clubs Canadiens de Québec et Montréal dont les représentants sont parmi nous aujourd'hui. Je voudrais donc acceuillir chaleureusement leurs membres qui sont ici présents.

My pleasure at being with you tonight is heightened by the nature of the occasion which has brought us here – the Biennial Conference of the Association of Canadian Clubs. I am happy to have had a pretty close connection with the Canadian Club movement for a long time. I believe in it. It has often been pointed out that the clubs form the only organization in Canada that exists for the primary, indeed the sole, purpose of promoting a faith in our country and a love for it. There are now, I am told, some seventy Canadian Clubs with 30,000 members. Our debt to them is immense.

At one of the earliest meetings of the first club, in Hamilton, just over seventy years ago, a motion was passed which I will quote in part: 'that it is . . . a fit and proper time to take definite steps . . . to deepen and widen the regard of Canadians for their land of birth or adoption. . . .' These words might well be repeated today. I will say more about this a little later on.

This Canadian Club gathering is appropriate as regards both time and place. Every schoolboy ought to know why. But I wonder whether he does, for, alas, we don't help our children to know as much as they should about our own history. For instance, would the Charlottetown Conference of 1864 ring a bell in their juvenile minds, or the names of the men who took part in it? I fear not, and, if I am right, that cannot be regarded as a tribute to those who direct our school systems.

You will remember the story of how the conference began. It was to have been a meeting of delegates from the three Maritime Provinces to discuss the possibility of their union. It was to be a cosy Maritime affair. But, to use a term that would have been unknown then, the Canadian delegation in a sense 'gate-crashed'. The Canadians were doubtful about their reception; the Maritimers were not unfriendly, but rather bewildered by their arrival. As the members of the three delegations arrived from New Brunswick, Nova Scotia, and the Canadas, there was no one on hand to meet them except a solitary minister. He managed to welcome two of the three groups, in the case of the Canadians going out to meet them in a little boat all by himself. He deserves a place in history.

Why was there no reception committee for the visitors? You may know the reason. For the first time in twenty-one years there was a circus in Charlottetown, and everybody from miles around had come to see it. Perhaps that event, with the festive atmosphere it created, helped to give the conference an auspicious start. At any rate, the Canadian delegates were welcomed and permitted to present their case for confederation.

In this, John Macdonald played the major part. It is not belittling those great Canadians George Brown and George Cartier, and their colleagues from other parts of what became Canada, to say that Sir John A. Macdonald was the principal architect of the Canadian nation as we know it. But could any outstanding statesman in a national history be treated with greater neglect? Unlike those of many figures in our story, Macdonald's name has not been commemorated even in Canada's capital (although before long the Macdonald-Cartier bridge across the Ottawa River will mark one of the great, fruitful partnerships that have occurred from time to time between men of French and English race). In the United States the birthday of Abraham Lincoln is reverently celebrated each year. Lincoln and what he did to save the Union are enshrined in the thought and feeling of the American people. Macdonald's service to Canada was different in kind but not in degree, for without him we would not have had the creation of a Canadian nation, nor would its preservation have been achieved. I would like to see Macdonald's birthday established as a fixture in our national calendar.

May I return to the Canadian Clubs? We are reminded tonight, as I mentioned before, of the beginning of the movement. The young men who conceived it didn't hold a great banquet at the beginning, with florid speeches and a prodigious bill of fare – their organizing meeting took place one evening in the austere atmosphere of a business office. One can picture the setting – writing machines, roll-top desks, a letter-press. But this did not matter. The young men had what the Quakers call 'concern' – concern for the future of their country, and the danger that it might accept the views of Goldwin Smith and others, who preached a gospel of negation: that Canada should accept extinction, renounce all belief in what she could do as an independent country, and choose to be absorbed in a continental United States.

The young men who met in Hamilton in 1892 had cause for concern. Their country was in the throes of a great depression, but their talk was not about tariffs and exports – it was about the spirit of the country they belonged to. Since its beginning, the flame of patriotism had never burnt so low. The young men knew that what the nation needed was belief in itself, something which underlies even economics. The object of their thinking was, as they expressed it later, 'the deep importance to Canada of the cultivation of a spirit of patriotism in the hearts of her people'. Such a sentiment seems fitting and even urgent today.

Between 1892 and 1964 there are, of course, great differences. In the earlier years, as I said, we were in the grip of a severe depression. That is now far from true, but without, I hope, seeming too pessimistic, I suggest that there appears to be this in common between the two periods: a diminished faith in the country to which we belong. Our present material well-being has not restored our confidence in ourselves. In the Litany there appears a supplication which reads in part: 'In all times of prosperity . . . Good Lord deliver us.' It is worth remembering.

Historians, I am sure, will point to the early 1960s as a time of doubt about our future as a nation, when we were subject to dangerously heavy constitutional and emotional strains; when the very structure of our national life was questioned; when people were prepared to ask whether the Canadian experiment was worth while; when union with a more powerful neighbour was talked about with a freedom that would have been looked on as treason in former years; when the cynics and the faint-hearted dared to belittle the deeds of their fathers and instil doubts in their sons.

We are often told that Canada is, after all, an artificial country. So it is. All the more credit to the men who built it. All building is artificial, and so are all national economies. Building always demands a price. We have been prepared to pay the price because we have believed that there was something infinitely precious to preserve, and that the cost of preservation was not too high. Although natural geographical lines in North America, as we know, run north and south, we, since the beginning, have been determined to establish ties between east and west to maintain and strengthen our national unity – railways, air lines, radio, television, highways, microwave, and most recently a chain of cultural centres.

If the maintenance of our east and west links is questioned as a national policy, the doubters are men who fail to understand the land in which they live. I venture to assert that our mental and emotional difficulties as Canadians are aggravated because too few of us remember what really gives our national life its meaning. Too many of us have lost the concept of Canada. Our forebears understood it in 1864. Present-day education has failed, failed signally, to teach us what kind of country Canada is. We are, at the moment, celebrating the centenary of the Charlottetown Conference of 1864, and we are preparing to commemorate fittingly a century of Confederation – the greatest event so far in our national story. At the same time there are, as I say, among our people those who argue that Canada cannot endure. Could there be a greater paradox? Absurdities, minor though they may be, appear from time to time in the context of our centenary celebrations, which reflect curiously on our thinking. For example, in a town in the Niagara Peninsula, not far from the scene of the Battle of Queenston Heights, which can be said to have kept Canada Canadian, it was suggested that an American firm be asked to submit plans for our centennial event!

[7]

I wonder whether those who light-heartedly talk about a
political union between ourselves and the United States realize
how many are the differences between us. There are, of course,
also many things which we and they have in common – deep
principles on which our two countries were founded, as well
as innumerable superficial resemblances; and there are many
things we can learn from our neighbours. All this is obvious;
but there *are* differences. If there were not, the reasons for our
separate existence would almost disappear. One profound difference lies in our forms of government. They are both essentially
democratic, but how unlike they are! The parliamentary
system, surmounted by the Crown, which we have inherited,
cherished, and adapted to a federal constitution, is not, of
course, perfect – no type of government is; but I can think of
no system that makes an administration more flexible and more
responsive to the will of the people. There is no chance, under
our plan, of a deadlock between the administration and the
legislature. If there is a jam between them, either the legislature
replaces the administration or the administration asks the
electorate for another legislature.

If we take the trouble to think about it, we can list many
things that distinguish us from our neighbours, such as the
administration of law in Canada and the status of our judiciary.
Other differences have often been listed, but I fear just as often
forgotten. Owing to the operation of the two forms of government, we have numerous measures which the Americans have
not, such as non-contributory old-age pensions, family allowances, public hospital insurance, workmen's compensation on a
state basis, a national system of unemployment insurance. Other
features of our life, perhaps harder to analyse, are involved in
such comparisons. The operation of the parliamentary and
congressional systems of government are partly responsible
for this. They promote different habits of thought. There may

[8]

seem often to be little to distinguish individual Canadians from their opposite numbers across the border, but if you put a hundred Americans in one room and a hundred Canadians in another and place before each group fundamental questions on which they should have views, I think you would find striking differences between the collective opinions of the two. The result of such an examination would not lessen our confidence in our own country.

The greatest contrast, of course, between the American nation and ours is that the United States is a country of one language and one culture and Canada is a country of two languages and basically two cultures. Let me say quite frankly and humbly that it has taken us in English-speaking Canada a long time to realize that there *are* two cultures in this country and that our French-speaking fellow-citizens were here first. How much were I and my contemporaries taught at school about the achievements of the French régime in Canada? Were we led to think of Champlain or Brébeuf, of Frontenac or Laval, as being among the makers of our homeland? Too often the history we learned seemed to have started in 1759, and let me say, if I may, that on the other hand our French-speaking fellow-citizens were often given the impression that Canadian history stopped in the same year. In the schools I attended, it is true that French was taught, but exactly as was Latin – as another dead language. No boy or girl could emerge from such schools able to speak French, however much grammar they might have crammed for exams. Was there any effort to have it given us by persons whose mother tongue was French? No. It was taught, in earlier years at least, by English-speaking teachers whose accent, in most cases, would have caused a shudder in Quebec or Paris. On certain occasions we sang 'The Maple Leaf Forever', which we hoped would 'the thistle, shamrock, rose entwine'. Much we owe to them all, *but* – was the *fleur de lis*

[9]

part of the garland? No – not at least in the original version. What we heard about Quebec might have come from a picture postcard; the history of French Canada described the life of a people strangely remote from our own.

I am now talking about the past. Many changes have taken place in the last few years. In numerous provincial schools in Ontario, French is no longer entrusted entirely to English-speaking instructors, but is beginning to be placed in the hands of well-selected teachers whose mother tongue is French. A straw in the wind is the recent establishment in Toronto of a French school, in which the pupils are taught in, and are thus familiarized with, Canada's other language. Such changes do not apply only to the education of children but to their parents also, who are taking an interest in learning French today which would have been inconceivable fifteen, ten, or even five years ago. I am thinking of the classes in French organized by English-speaking business firms, and of many other developments which show an increasing recognition of the fact that we have two national languages in Canada – English and French.

It must, of course, be remembered that more than a quarter of our population comes of neither French nor British stock. We welcome the cultures which these people have brought with them; we value the rich contribution they make to our national life. We, however, have two founding races, French and English in origin, their languages and cultures having a special and permanent place in the national scene. That is an historical fact, not a political judgment.

I firmly believe that the majority of people in both French- and English-speaking Canada desire to work together for the well-being of their country, but there are extremists – how well we know it! – and extremists on each side reproduce their kind on the other. It is their harsh voices we hear too often. If irresponsible speeches are made, they are faithfully reported;

if acts of violence take place, we hear all about them; if, for instance, some fanatical young men destroy a monument to Wolfe in Quebec, we are told about it in full detail. Sensation sells well. If, however, some observations are made, on either side of the Ottawa River, in support of moderation and tolerance, such statements are frequently overlooked.

Yet let me remind you that tolerance is a characteristic Canadian virtue, fully shared by both races, and that it is a feature of our life that has given us our finest spiritual tradition. If I seem to be talking in easy platitudes, consider what other nations think of Canada. From my own experience I think I know, and others with similar opportunities will, I am sure, agree. We possess the qualities of moderation, forbearance, and a sense of compromise, which give us a maturity beyond our years. This may sound smug; I believe it to be true. If it had not been for these qualities, we would not have survived as a nation today. Canada, indeed, is the product of tolerance. She is a veritable school of tolerance, and let us remind ourselves of what tolerance means. It does not mean indifference. It means your respect for the other man's point of view while you hold firmly to your own.

In the argument that is now going on, we may well deplore the voices that are raised here and there in English-speaking Canada in tones of irritation and impatience over what some persons have said – always in a minority, let us remember – in French-speaking Canada. But if there ever was a time for patience and restraint it is now. If, without patience (on both sides), we reach an impasse, there will be no retreat. But to urge patience is not to advocate silence. In Canada individuals often suffer from a reluctance to state their views, to say what they think. It is so easy for us, when confronted by some controversial subject, to declare an unwillingness to get mixed up in the controversy. But we should all get 'mixed up' in discussions of great issues. If more moderate men would talk and could be heard in this national debate, we would move surely, and perhaps even swiftly, towards a solution of our problems. The citizen's duty is to participate. Our problems will not all be solved by laws or regulations, although some matters, of course, must be dealt with by legislation. That was true of the use of the French language on our currency and our postage stamps. Such innovations, however, have never impressed many French-speaking Canadians. These so-called (and wrongly termed) 'concessions' were, after all, decided on grudgingly and often after acrimonious debate. What is most important, supremely important, does not lie in the field of the printed word, but in the sphere of the intangible; and a solution for these problems can come only through a change in our thinking – I could almost call it a mental revolution. The malaise in Quebec cannot easily be defined, but it exists, and we know, or should know, why; we, all of us, French- and English-speaking, are paying the price now for our attitudes in former years.

The great debate goes on. Honest deliberations, discussions, and arguments in a free society are healthy, but not so violence in deed, or intemperance in words. French-speaking Canada and English-speaking Canada are marked by numerous striking differences – differences that make our country interesting and enrich it. Underlying these contrasts, we have the deeper things in common. Trace back the civilizations inherited by both French- and English-speaking Canada centuries ago, and you will find common roots.

I have told you what I feel, and feel deeply, about this crisis in our national life – and crisis is not too strong a word. I know we will surmount it, but, if I may repeat myself, let me say that a condition of success is a real comprehension of the country in which we live.

Sir Robert Borden once made a remark of deep significance.

This is what he said: 'We must decide whether a spirit of Canadianism or of continentalism is to prevail on the northern half of this continent.' That question has been asked and answered at more than one moment in our history. The answer comes naturally if we are aware of the 'spirit of Canadianism'. But there are continentalists among us today. To defeat them, we need to know the character of Canada, its uniqueness as a nation – because it is unique. Geographically, racially, politically, it is unlike any other country in the world. We need to recognize the sacred duty of preserving it and giving it unity. I am not thinking of this only in terms of language. We should, of course, have a more general knowledge of both tongues, but it would be unrealistic ever to expect all Canadians to be familiar with both French and English. We shall achieve unity when all of us, whoever we are, take pride in the accomplishments of Canadians irrespective of race or time or place – when boys and girls in Fredericton can be thrilled by the journeys of La Vérendrye, or a child in Chicoutimi can find excitement in the exploits of David Thompson. We must sternly rebuke those who would rend Canada asunder. We must arouse those who would stand idly by and watch it fall apart. We must comprehend the majesty of Canada, the glory of Canada – yes – the greatness of Canada. These terms are not too extravagant. They are a just tribute to the men who made what we inherit. They knew in the 1860s what Canada was to be; they set themselves on the road with conviction and courage. It is for us to recapture their spirit – the spirit of the men who saw our country in practical terms together with those who sensed its romance. It is for us to be worthy of the men of Confederation. Pray God it may be so.

An Introduction
to Canada

An address at the opening session of H.R.H. The Duke of Edinburgh's
Second Commonwealth Study Conference, at the University
of Montreal, May 15, 1962. The members of the
conference numbered 300 and came from
thirty-four Commonwealth countries
and territories.

I SHALL TRY this morning to give you a brief introduction to the country in which you will be living for the next few weeks, and tell you something of the land which is to be the scene of your studies.

Those of you who are coming to Canada for the first time will find that we possess a complicated national pattern. We Canadians give much thought to this. In few countries are the citizens so much concerned with the understanding of themselves; this is, I think, a healthy exercise. If you find it difficult to get a clear picture of the land you are visiting, you can be comforted by the fact that you may perhaps share certain perplexities with its own inhabitants!

Nous nous réunissons aujourd'hui dans une des plus grandes villes du monde où l'on parle français. Permettez-moi, en employant une de nos deux langues nationales, de souhaiter, aux membres de cette conférence qui parlent français, un accueil cordial et sincère.

To those of you who do not know this country, and I take it that means most of you, I would not venture to suggest precisely what you may expect to see. I would, however, hazard two guesses.

My first guess is that you will find the primary problems that

[17]

Canadians face in today's society to be much more familiar, far closer to your own experience, than you may have thought possible. The communities of the Commonwealth are feeling the impact of industrialization at a pace not even dreamed of a generation ago, let alone in the distant era of the first industrial revolution. We are all of us living in what has been called the scientific revolution. Ours is a world of instantaneous communications, swift travel, and easy transport of materials; of an industrial chemistry that will soon be able to make almost anything out of anything else. It is a world of automation, of electronics and atomic energy, with the need for highly skilled and intelligent workers. It is also a world whose population grows by millions every month. High pressure is thus brought to bear on the most precious elements – land and water, the supply of which is not unlimited even in Canada.

In spite of the many social and political differences among us, and the various approaches to industrialization in our countries, we have each of us far more in common with one another than with our grandfathers or with the world of 1914 or even of 1939. Science and technology are universal languages, and we are all moving in the same direction. What you will see, then, of the conditions and the problems faced by a new mine manager in the wilderness of northern Quebec, or by a self-employed farmer on the prairies, or by a semi-skilled labourer in an old urban industry adopting automation, will not be so very unfamiliar to you. These conditions and problems will, indeed, have a great deal in common with those met by a hydro engineer in Pakistan or a cocoa-planter from Ghana or a trade-union organizer from Kuala Lumpur. In this field, therefore – the one with which this Conference is primarily concerned – you will find in Canada much that is surprisingly familiar. You will discover the sad mistakes we have sometimes made, and you will understand what we have been able to achieve in the battle against those new industrial forces which, if we let them, can dehumanize men and rob them of their dignity. Thus, by looking at Canada, you will also be discovering and understanding *your* problems; and you may perhaps leave here somewhat better prepared to comprehend and benefit from the things that industrialization is doing for human beings in other lands.

I would hazard another guess about your expectations.

Canada has been fortunate in having many friends. Indeed we possess no traditional enemies; we have never had colonies but have evolved from colonial status ourselves; we are not charged with the great responsibilities of defence and power; we represent an alternative North American pathway to industrial prosperity; we can be said to be a different kind of American nation. We have sometimes won from other peoples a vague feeling of goodwill, or even admiration, which is not always hard-earned or fully deserved.

I think you may well find in this country much that will puzzle and surprise you or may lead you to jump to false conclusions. There are things – perhaps not particularly striking or sensational – that are peculiarly Canadian. They require some effort to know. And they must be taken into account, if a misunderstanding of this country is to be avoided and hence in part a misunderstanding of the deeper problems with which we are all concerned at this Conference. So if those of you who know Canada well will bear with me, I shall try to point out what I think are certain essential and peculiar features of our Canadian society. I do not do so by way of excuse, in the sense that to understand all is to pardon all; nor, on the other hand, shall I try to list our shortcomings by way of penance. I do so, rather, in order that you may see a little more objectively the community in which you will be living for the next few weeks.

In the first place, Canada is a northern country. It is the

largest nation in the world whose economic and social rhythms are guided by a northern geography. This is such an obvious fact that it is often discounted. It cannot be ignored. The effect of temperatures below the freezing-point, and often sub-zero, for many months of the year has had a crucial effect on the sort of buildings and roads we must create, on the kinds and amounts of food we must grow and consume, on our clothing and other necessities, and, ultimately, on the sort of people we are. To give some rather trivial but perhaps telling examples, I doubt if there is any large metropolis in the world, except possibly Moscow, that faces an annual problem of snow removal as serious as that of Montreal.

Our steel plants must often dynamite their frozen piles of iron ore in winter in order that it may be used in the blast-furnaces. Our great inland waterway, the St. Lawrence–Great Lakes system, on which our history has hinged so critically for over three hundred years, and which still carries the greatest volume of our goods, is useless to navigation for one-third of the year. Conversely, the extreme summer heat also creates its problems. To give you some notion of the possible range of climate in Canada, our national capital annually records high and low temperatures with a spread of as much as 125 Fahrenheit degrees between them.

Closely connected with the difficulty of climatic extremes are the problems presented by the rigours of Canada's topography. We have great areas of rich soil, but much of our land is either muskeg or permafrost hitherto impossible to settle or even traverse; or else it is the immensity of rock, which has yielded a wealth of fur, timber, and minerals but is unsuitable for more than sparse and scattered human settlement. One historian has chosen to describe Canada in stark terms as a vast hinterland exploited for a few staples from the narrow base of the St. Lawrence and the lower Great Lakes, the Saskatchewan River valleys, and the Fraser River delta, where the great mass of its population lives. A similar observation could well be made about the Maritime Provinces. Their pioneers, however, were fishermen seeking new fishing-grounds or seamen-farmers in quest of new pastures. This has been true ever since the Vikings touched our north-eastern shores a thousand years ago.

Unlike the nation to our south with its richer soil and milder climate, we have not been able fully to occupy our vast territories. We have moved in and out of them with the rhythm of the seasons. Except in the few, thin, densely-peopled southern areas, we have been travellers, traders, and gatherers-in, not permanent settlers and residents. Our hinterland has depended almost completely, in a way that the more self-sufficient American frontier did not, upon the economic and political support of the metropolitan centres of Europe and of such major cities as Montreal and Toronto. You will also become keenly aware as you travel through our Dominion of the striking manner in which the great regions divide Canadians from one another and give each a different type of environment to cope with and different natural resources to draw upon, and, I may add, lend variety and interest to the Canadian scene: the Maritime Provinces, two large islands and two peninsulas riding far out into the North Atlantic; the vast shield of the world's oldest rock in northern Quebec and Ontario; the expanse of the central prairies; the western mountain regions; and the strip of Pacific Coast country with its softer climate and giant forests.

The physical difficulties and complexities of this land have deeply affected our national character and history. They have made great virtues out of some of the sterner human qualities – frugality and caution, discipline and endurance. Geography, perhaps even more than the influence of the churches, has made us puritans.

Canada has often been called a young country. In this fourth century of settlement, and close to the hundredth year of the Dominion's creation, we can hardly be described as very young. Unformed, in many ways even now undeveloped, still open to unknown possibilities – yes. We are all these things because of the character of our environment and the way we depend upon it for a living, but not because in relation to the newer countries of the world we have a short history. Nor are we without political maturity.

Nature for us has usually been an enemy, symbolized by the terrifying spirit-creature that the fur-traders told about as having been encountered in the forests of the trackless north. Or, if not an enemy, nature has been a source of bounty to be treated with awe. She has rarely been something to be tamed or enjoyed. At best we might exploit her quickly and move on. It is little wonder that the atmosphere of our towns still often suggests that of the mining-camp or the logging-drive. All too often we have not built for beauty or permanence. Even our largest communities still have about them, certainly in the outskirts, something of the air of sleeping-compounds or trading-posts. Our cities and towns too often are unworthy of the splendid countryside in which they have been built. We are apt to enjoy looking at architecture chiefly when it is being put up or pulled down. Perhaps it is because we have such a vast amount of land that it has been as yet little measured by the imagination, however accurately and often it and its gross national product have been measured by the Bureau of Statistics.

We have not, until the revolution that has just begun to overtake us at mid century, been much concerned to foster the arts. But it is true that in the past decade there have been some hopeful developments. A few years ago a public body was set up free of governmental interference and with a substantial endowment for the purpose of fostering scholarship, the arts, and literature. Of our marked progress in these fields, the

Canada Council is both a symbol and an instrument.

Signs of a new growth in the arts, however, leave us little cause for complacency as long as we neglect the study of the environment. We have often ignored the long-term aesthetic and social needs of town-planning in order to pursue immediate economic ends. We have not given to our communities the fine squares and noble public buildings and pleasant urban parks which belong to peoples who have known better how to embellish life, but have surrendered too fully to those means of transportation upon which of course our livelihood and survival have depended. In a way perhaps unsurpassed even in the United States, we have worshipped first the railway and then the automobile. When we were experiencing our first heady decade of real prosperity some fifty years ago – and most Canadians agreed with the prime minister of the day who told us that the new century belonged to Canada – we built not only one transcontinental railway but in addition projected two others for which we were not ready. We have been paying for our false optimism ever since. But now we face the even heavier monetary and human cost imposed by the North American idolatry of the motor car.

What transportation and construction will do to our urban scene is by no means settled yet. Much the most important phase of our industrialization belongs to the past twenty years. There are striking signs of our economic growth in the nineteen-fifties – such as the creation of the giant seaway for shipping and power on the St. Lawrence River and the construction of the pipelines to carry the newly discovered western oil and gas across Canada. Close to 20,000 miles of these have been built within this country in the last ten years. The pipeline is often referred to as the 'prime mover' of the present day, just as was the railway in the last century. Engineers tell us that oil and gas pipelines may be joined in the next decade by those carrying solids. I think it true to say that the pipeline is transforming Canadian transportation.

The biggest changes are yet to come. Within the next two generations we shall probably undertake as much new building as there has been in this country since the beginning. Our secondary and service industries are expected to take corresponding strides forward. And we have begun to face the problem of fostering the human resources which we have often neglected in the past. But the full powers of an industrial society are still before us. To a degree not found in more industrialized nations, we still have it within us to decide what kind of society we are to be and how we may guide the economic and cultural revolution we have begun to face.

We must approach it in our own way. When you examine some of the peculiarly Canadian aspects of the two identities we rather loosely call Business and Labour, you will discover that they are in some degree of contrast with what we find in the United States. 'Prudence' and 'moderation' are words that come readily to mind when one thinks of financial and industrial concerns in this country. There is a Lowland Scots canniness and common sense about their directors and senior officers. Perhaps I should add that these qualities have sometimes been linked by critics with a lack of boldness and imagination and of the will to live dangerously. Young men in Canadian business move from firm to firm or from industry to industry less frequently than do their American counterparts.

The Canadian investor is also conservative, and he tends to prefer enterprises whose common stocks have something of the security of government bonds. Indeed, he is inclined to prefer bonds and life insurance (we are relatively the most heavily insured people in the world) to any investments, however attractive, involving a large element of risk. I except, of course, the great volume of highly speculative bets placed on the most volatile of mining stocks, which a sociologist might describe as the Canadian equivalent of football pools or national sweepstakes.

One result of this caution and of the limited amount of money for investment available in Canada is that the great majority of ventures requiring large quantities of capital have been undertaken by non-Canadians – particularly, in this century, by Americans. The influx of capital from the United States, and with it the American entrepreneurs who often come to settle permanently here, has been of immense economic benefit to this country. Canadians have frequently expressed the fear that such a boon was being purchased at the cost of future political independence. But the historian surveying such American economic influences over the past century or so seems to have good reason for drawing the opposite conclusion: that the financial and industrial stimulus we have thus received may well have been one of those things that have enabled us to assert our *political* independence so effectively.

Something of a parallel can be seen in the history of the labour movement in Canada. In the early days of our industrialization our labour unions drew much on the experience and knowledge of the British unions and the British labour movement. Inevitably, however, and under much the same influences as those to which I referred a moment ago in the movement of capital, Canadian labour turned more and more for help to the great American trade unions. Thus many Canadian unions are part of international bodies whose headquarters are in the United States and who still exercise some degree of influence or control. An example is the very powerful steelworkers' union. It is worth noting that its Canadian national office, with its excellent equipment for research and its professional staff, provides for Canadian locals the leadership which originally had to come from outside if there was to be any union organization in steel at all. In other industries, such as automobile manufacturing and non-ferrous metals, where ownership and control reside largely in American parent companies, the Canadian unions have found that membership in the international was the most effective way to gain an adequate bargaining position. I should also add that most Canadian unions, whether they have an international connection or not, derive great strength and some sense of identity and common purpose from their membership in the Canadian Labour Congress. And I should point out that the Confédération des Syndicats Nationaux, chiefly French-speaking, has been a major force in the province of Quebec.

There are also many differences, but it is the similarities between American and Canadian labour that are most significant. Like American union members and unlike those almost everywhere else, Canadian workers have not thought of themselves as a single class, nor have they reacted as a class to fundamental issues. They have been much more likely to regard themselves not as producers but as consumers and as owners. Nor has there been, in the strictly European sense of the word, a *bourgeoisie* for them to react against. There are no clearly defined class divisions in Canadian society. Instead of class conflict, sectional and religious differences have supplied most of the matter for our social and political arguments.

These considerations lead directly to the central facts of our political life. Unlike the other nations in this hemisphere, Canada has no revolutionary tradition. Existence was too precarious and too dependent upon the merchants and administrators and soldiers sent out from the imperial centres of Paris and London to allow for revolution. This trend was strongly reinforced by the conservatism of the early settlers. Those of French origin stoutly rejected both the American and the French revolutions and all their works. The English-speaking refugees from the rebellious Thirteen Colonies went north in order to live in a country that would still be ruled by British law and social custom.

The appeal of later would-be revolutionaries to such a population was extremely limited, especially when the restless or dissatisfied could so easily cross the border. Canada, in fact, has been from the beginning a stopping-point for millions of Europeans on their journey to the hoped-for prosperity of the United States. Even now there are at least as many Canadian-born persons living there as the total population of several of our provinces. Meanwhile fresh waves of foreign immigration have been moving into Canada. Since the end of the Second World War, the number of new arrivals has equalled nearly one-seventh of our total population. The mobility of our people, both within the country and across our borders, is extremely high; Canadians, new and old alike, change their place of residence on the average every six years. On the other hand, there is no doubt that there are many Canadians who are all too immobile: men and women who because of their age or limited education or other handicaps are unable to move from one industry or one town to another. These are the stranded victims of rapid industrialization. But their plight is not peculiarly Canadian.

To look at another aspect of Canadian conservatism, we present an image of the frontier radically different from the more familiar one to the south of us. Unlike the American wild west, western Canada was planned and ordered by government and large private corporations in advance of settlement. Since the mid nineteenth century it has been dominated by priest and mounted policeman, Hudson's Bay factor and bank manager, rather than by sheriff's posse or self-sufficient pioneer. The company town, often isolated in the wilderness and based on a single industry, with company and union assuming many communal responsibilities, has been an important part of this pattern.

The large-scale, carefully planned enterprise, dominating its field and aided by government regulation and support, is typical of our whole development. The stories of the Hudson's Bay Company, the Canadian Pacific Railway, the great metal monopolies, run through our history. It is hard to conceive of mid-twentieth-century Canada without the Crown corporations, those semi-independent governmental bodies containing features of both public and private enterprise. The device of the Crown corporation has been used to manage our largest railway system, to develop hydro-electric power, to market Canadian wheat, to administer the nation's major shipping harbours, to create a profitable petro-chemical industry, a national research council, a national film-producing unit, and a great passenger air service. It has been used to build and maintain the Canadian Broadcasting Corporation, which is not only one of the largest but also, in terms of its productions, one of the finest radio and television networks in the world. The Crown corporation has been used, as in the Second World War when over seventy of them were created to meet the needs of war production, to undertake tasks which private capital would not or should not be responsible for, yet which are better handled outside the organization of government. In spite of the huge measure of state enterprise represented by these Crown corporations, such terms as 'public control' or 'government planning' still arouse suspicion in the minds of many Canadians. Hence these government bodies have grown in a typically Canadian manner—for practical rather than ideological reasons. And, finally, they illustrate the way in which the stark facts of geography and the bias of our history have shaped our thinking and our institutions.

The Canadian constitution, what little there is of it in

written form, sets up the objectives of peace, order, and good government, rather than those of 'life, liberty, and the pursuit of happiness'. As the historian William Morton has pointed out, we are a society that is founded on the principle of allegiance rather than of social contract, on the organic growth of tradition itself rather than by an explicit act of reason or will. One of the most fundamental but least obvious differences between our North American nation and its neighbour lies in this: that for Canadians the fact and principle of authority were established prior to the fact and principle of freedom.

This has been an advantage in a society like ours. Authority and allegiance under our monarchy have allowed us a wide diversity of customs and rights in a way that the rational scheme and abstractions of republican democracy could not. We are a plural community made up of two major and many minor cultural groups. There is no distinct, uniform, and overwhelmingly Canadian way of life into which new-comers are expected to be caught up and reshaped. Differences are welcomed. In our cultural and religious diversity, as in the federal structure of our government and in the conservative allegiance to authority that guarantees and holds together this diversity, we have been compared to the old Austro-Hungarian Empire. The comparison may sound odd; it has at least the virtue of making one look beneath that obvious gloss of North Americanism and discern those natural differences between ourselves and our neighbours which give our international border its meaning.

It suggests, too, that we may have much in common with the plural and diversified communities of other Commonwealth nations. For, like Canada, they were formed by practical compromise through a process of historical evolution, rather than by the application of logic. Independence through the growth of responsible government was still, in 1960 in Nigeria and in 1961 in Tanganyika, being adapted to the needs of the Commonwealth's growing number of diverse communities. This process was first seen here in Canada a century ago.

Most Canadians are proudly conscious of the fact that next to Great Britain we are the oldest nation in the Commonwealth. We hope we have learned the lessons which diversity must teach a people; but, in spite of the sincere warmth and affection with which I know you will be received wherever you go in Canada, you may discover hidden pockets of sentiment contrasting sharply with the tolerance which I believe to be characteristic of the great majority of Canadians. You may well run across the sort of person who is moved to look unsympathetically on our immigrants – in spite of the fact that his own ancestors were not exactly original members of society. There is, however, no question that our new Canadians are making an essential and vastly important contribution to Canadian life.

Our experience of the plural society has been real and searching. But even its limited successes were not easily a-chieved. As the novelist Hugh MacLennan has put it, 'Not only was this country formed out of the flotsam and jetsam of three or four defeated racial and political groups; some of these groups had once been bitter enemies of one another. But they *had* to live here, and they *had* to live in peace with one another.' The cost of doing so has been high. We have had to do without a very clear image of ourselves, without a national culture, in the sense that these are to be found in Europe and the United States. The majority of Canadians are still not capable of speaking both our official languages (although in the last few years, happily, there has begun a ground-swell of feeling and action to overcome this neglect), and a sizeable number of Canadians from the minority groups have not yet learned either language.

In our politics the sword-play of ideas, real intellectual debate, has been a luxury that we have often had to do without, if we were going to hold together at all. Our loose federal constitutional structure, with immense powers vested in the provinces, has made it very difficult to tackle many new problems; I refer particularly to those that come from rapid industrialization – problems that are national in scope, but provincial in constitutional terms. The province of Quebec, in particular, represents not just one of ten local governments. It stands, with the strong emotion of conviction in the minds of French-speaking Canadians, as the symbol of French culture in North America. It has taken the English-speaking majority many generations to accept that fact – not grudgingly or indifferently, but proudly, as a mark of the rich variety of our national life.

Lastly, we can never forget that always, with all our compromises and frustrations as a small country in everything but geography, we have to live next door to the most powerful nation on earth. As a result of this, one Canadian has ventured to say, with more humour than accuracy, that we are a people bounded on one side by the northern lights and on the other by an inferiority complex just as vivid. The vast influence of American culture is now beginning to reach all of you as strongly as it has affected us for many generations. Like us you recognize the success and the ability of the Americans at so many things, and their generosity and goodwill. Canadians are sometimes critical of their neighbours. But, if we would only admit it, each of us in our own way possesses some unattractive habits and traits. What is important is to acknowledge and accept, gladly and without jealousy, the best things into our own lives from wherever they come. In the end we can each of us realize our own true national individuality by first searching out what is good and only secondly inquiring into its origin.

If I had to sum up the lesson of the Canadian experience – in living with ourselves, in living with the Americans, in adapting to our needs our European inheritance, and in responding to the demands of a northern environment – I should put it like this: the life of a nation, like that of an individual, is not something to be lived in the innocent and happy illusion that other people can be made to like us, or to resemble us, but something to be endured on a basis of reality. The big problems are not ones which can really ever be settled and 'fixed' by some magic formula, some act of revolution, some political system. They are the problems we must teach ourselves to live with, just as all peoples, for the first time in human history, are now simply forced to learn to live with one another, if we are to survive at all. So perhaps at last the lesson of the Canadian experiment has become relevant not just for ourselves but for others. Canadians have had to outgrow, first, a pro-French or pro-British colonial attitude, a mixture of pride and subservience, and then, later, a tough nationalist assertiveness. But our experience has meant, at its best, these past three centuries and more, something deeper than either the obverse or the reverse of the colonial mentality. It has created 'a common psychology of endurance and survival', an ability to accept compromise and illogical variety and even at times a sense of inferiority or defeat, and, in the end, to transcend them.

Just as I think this country because of its experience has a role to play in the world community, so has the family of nations to which we belong. The question of whether the existence of the Commonwealth has much bearing on the great matters of war and peace has often been asked. I do not intend to argue the point now. But I would like to repeat something said recently by one of our most respected diplomatists. He suggested that the Commonwealth's course is not set one way or another but that its role and function depend heavily at any given time on a conscious act of will on the part of all of us. 'I believe', he said, 'that there is a reality in the personal relationships in diplomacy among Commonwealth countries.

At the risk of sounding theological, I believe it because I have experienced it. At least', he continued, 'there is a reality for believers.'

It seems to me that this Conference is an example of an act of will, of a decision to stay in touch with one another, to trust one another, to work together as a community. I believe the Commonwealth is an association which is moving towards a fuller agreement on the few great moral issues that really matter.

We Canadians find ourselves happy as one of its senior members. This Conference brings home to us its nature and genius. It would, I think, be quite impossible to assemble representatives of thirty-four countries and territories whose relations were those of foreign states in a gathering as intimate and informal as this one. Our membership in the Commonwealth makes it possible. Our Conference will, I have no doubt, achieve its primary purpose, but it will do something else as well. It will help to bring Commonwealth countries closer together. It will help to strengthen those bonds of friendship among us which Edmund Burke described in a familiar phrase as 'light as air but strong as links of iron'. If this be true, none could be happier than your Canadian hosts.

Comment on
'The Dialogue'

An address delivered at the Convocation of
Carleton University, Ottawa,
May 24, 1963.

LORD DUFFERIN said that retired governors-general were like volcanoes – erupting occasionally and unexpectedly. But in his day a retired governor-general retired, as a rule, not only from office but from Canada. A Canadian released from this post, where frankness must always walk with the guardian angel of discretion, might prefer to quote another Victorian – Gladstone – who, cast out by Oxford and translated to Liverpool, began, 'At last, my friends I am come amongst you. And I am come unmuzzled.' But I am misleading you with fiery metaphors – the eruptions of this unmuzzled volcano are not dangerous; I only hope they may not be tedious.

I have always been greatly interested in this university. Its history has been short but vivid; histories needn't be long to be exciting. It was, I think, only about six years ago when you achieved university status. In a few days I am going to England to attend the celebration of the 700th anniversary of my college at Oxford; so there is quite a contrast in age between the two houses of learning. May I say a word about the older one? It will interest the women undergraduates of this university to know that I wouldn't be going to the celebrations at Balliol if it had not been for a lady. Now you mustn't jump to conclusions! I hasten to say that the lady in question lived in the thirteenth century. Let me tell you briefly what she did for learning in her day. John Balliol, our founder – a great land-owner in the north of England – got into trouble with the Church, and in order to punish him for his misdeeds the Bishop of Durham (whose lands adjoined Balliol's) imposed severe penance on the offender and ordered him to perform a sub-stantial act of charity. That took the form of the establishment in Oxford of a hostel for poor scholars. This was the beginning of Balliol College seven hundred years ago. But John did not do the job properly. The college, or hall, as it was called then, was financially starved – the scholars, I may say, were given a modest allowance of eightpence a day. The future of the little institution was very doubtful until John Balliol's wife, who bore the very decorative name of the Lady Dervorguilla, de-cided she would put the hall on a sound financial foundation, and did so. Hers is an honoured name in the history of the College.

You bear a great name. We are often careless in Canada about the figures in our history who have helped to give form and substance to our nation. Guy Carleton was one of those, and the decision to call this university after him helps us to remember what he stood for and what he did. One of the diffi-culties of teaching Canadian history is that our great names are for the most part associated with statesmanship, which is diffi-cult to make sufficiently dramatic to fire the youthful mind; a soldier makes a stronger appeal to the young. Carleton – Lord Dorchester, as he became – although a distinguished soldier, we associate with two great events in nation-building: the Quebec Act of 1774, which stood for the principles of concili-ation and tolerance after the fighting was over, and the Consti-tutional Act of 1791, which set up representative government. His name is therefore emblazoned in the annals of Canada.

You were fortunate in being established at the very heart of the nation, here in her capital. You in your strategic position are able to further the causes for which Guy Carleton stood. Indeed, you have a great responsibility, because through your researches and your academic curricula must be reflected the composite, complicated life of our country.

In four years' time – a very short period – we must express by words and actions what we think about Canada. I must say that reflections on this theme are apt to produce more clichés than most subjects; there are dozens like 'appraisal of the past', 'challenge of the future', 'sober confidence', and so on. But clichés do represent truths – they are rather like coins that are well worn by much usage but are still legal tender.

What are we going to do on July 1, 1967? I know a good deal of thought is being given to the subject and it is not for me to discuss the programme of this great event, with which I have no official connection, but I might perhaps express one or two thoughts as a private citizen. We have had some experience of anniversaries in Canada in recent years. Some time ago I was in Saskatchewan during the celebration of its Golden Jubilee as a province. I was much impressed by the approach that was made to this event by both government and people. The planning had started years before. The anniversary was marked by the establishment of a fine museum in Regina, but also by activities all over the province. The public responded to the appeal and one could sense a very deep and real feeling of pride in what had been accomplished over the fifty years of Saskatchewan's history. At that time Alberta was celebrating the fiftieth anniversary of its foundation as a province. Unfortunately, I was unable to be there then, but later I saw some of the permanent monuments which the Jubilee moved Alberta to build–among them being the two splendid concert halls in Edmonton and Calgary. I must mention a centenary in which I was privileged to take some part – the hundredth anniversary of the establishment of the mainland colony of British Columbia. Here again there was a great public response to the importance of the occasion, and all over the province, in communities of all sizes, things were done which have served as a permanent commemoration of the event. I mention these provincial anniversaries because I think they can suggest what can be done on a national scale four years from now. There are a few things that occur to me – not very original, perhaps, but I think appropriate to this occasion.

Our national capital must play a major part. That will call for, I think, large-scale ceremonial. As I have said before, ceremonial is a language in itself, and great ideas and deep feeling can be expressed through this medium. It so happens that we are very good at this in Canada. I hope that the coming celebrations will have as a central feature great and moving pageantry in the splendid setting of this city.

As we consider 1967, we can learn something from the Festival of Britain in 1951. Quite apart from what happened in London and the creation there of a great monument in the form of the Royal Festival Hall, there were very few communities all the way down to the smallest hamlet that did not make some effort to mark the event. Perhaps it was the renovation of the parish hall, the tidying up of the village green, the gift of a scholarship, the repair of an ancient church. Almost everywhere something was done to enrich the life of the community. All these are suggestions of what might be done here in 1967. In our programme or programmes we should include the restoration of surviving buildings (pathetically few in number) which belong to our past and lend it importance and dignity – structures which in addition to mere age have historical or architectural interest, or both. I don't know what thought has been given to the buildings of old Quebec in relation to the centenary. I know the city well, having lived there for a month each year for seven years, and, like many others, I have witnessed with distress the steady erosion of its beauty – despite gallant efforts to arrest the process.

So much for one aspect of the centenary. I wouldn't like to see omitted from the programme the element of fun – just fun. I don't think we Canadians can call ourselves a gay people, but on this great occasion it would be a happy thing if we could let ourselves go and, at least metaphorically speaking, 'dance in the streets'. I would suggest, however, that the growing of centennial beards might be dispensed with, like many other anniversary practices which have become, to use the language of the younger generation, a bit 'corny'.

But more important than the visible things we will be doing, either permanent or temporary, will be the encouragement the festival will give us to think about Canadian life. It should be an occasion for spiritual stock-taking – a time, as I have suggested, to ask ourselves, when we say 'I am a Canadian' what do we really mean; a time to ask, how can we deepen and strengthen the unity of our homeland? How often this word unity is used! If ever a word is well worn with use it is this. Let us be honest about this matter – we cannot claim that unity in this country has been really achieved. In fact, Confederation is subject today to greater strain than it has met for many years. We are now earnestly concerned about the relations between the two great races that created Canada, and thoughtful Canadians are asking how they can be improved. Much is said about what could be done through official inquiries, through legislation, through regulations of various kinds. I have no comments to make on this at all – many of the ideas that have been put forward are very important. But I would like to say this. The fundamental solution of our Canadian problem does not lie in documents, however helpful they may be. We will only achieve a full measure of unity when the people of Canada understand what it means, and desire it. It will come as a result of what you and I and eighteen million other people think and do. If we have the tolerance, the imagination, the foresight we need, then light will shine on the road ahead. There have been prejudices and mistakes and faults in both the great communities which are Canada. But I am talking today as an English-speaking Canadian, and I am very conscious of our errors in the past and in the present. May I give you a few examples of the loose and faulty thinking that one encounters.

When I was sitting with the Royal-Commission-with-the-long-name some years ago, in a Western city, the manager of the local radio station was telling us about the problem of languages in his broadcasting schedule. I asked him how many foreign languages he broadcast in. He said something like this: 'Well, there is German and Ukrainian and French . . .' I was obliged to remind him that French is not a foreign language in Canada – it was spoken in our country before English was. The remark was an innocent one made thoughtlessly, but while that kind of thing can happen we have not got a balanced and true approach to some major issues of the day.

I remember that when I was High Commissioner in London on two or three occasions several Canadian officers who were French-speaking asked to see me. One of them said, 'The relations between French and English in our army are very unsatisfactory. In fact, there are no relations except those of a purely professional nature.' He said that French-Canadian soldiers in his experience were full of appreciation of their reception in Great Britain and only wished that their fellow-Canadians would be as warm and understanding as the British public. This conversation occurred some years ago, but how far have we gone since then? This very year I was shocked, as I am sure many of you were, to hear that when road signs were put up in an Ontario city in our two national languages scores of protests were made at once by citizens in that area at the use of French in these notices. How often a French-speaking Canadian who is asked to fill in some government form has been told to use English; nothing could be more irritating to him, or more fundamentally wrong, or, if I may put it this way, more un-Canadian. We profess that in theory at least we are a bilingual country, but in practice bilingualism is marked only by certain moderate guarantees of French, such as apply to Parliament and the federal courts. How many English-speaking Canadians, however, fully accept the implications of the fact that in this country we have two different cultures existing side by side? This is imbedded in our foundations. Nevertheless, every measure leading to fuller biculturalism in Canada, such as the use of French and English on government cheques, has been attended by long and not always harmonious discussions, and the decision to use French in this way has often been finally accepted by those of the other language reluctantly and with little grace. That is not the way unity is achieved. I said a moment ago that French culture arrived first in Canada. It has been well said that Quebec is, in practice, a mother country itself – a homogeneous community guarding and perpetuating the fine traditions it has inherited; it is a bastion of French culture possessing strong ties with French-speaking Canadians wherever they live in Canada. It is right that this should be so.

A distinguished scholar in Quebec has said, 'Language is the key to my neighbour's house.' If all Canadians could speak both our national languages, the major problem of Canadian disunity might still exist, but bilingualism, if not a complete solution to this problem, would do much, very much, to enlarge that true dialogue between our two cultures which has been steadily maintained over the years by good Canadians, French-

[43]

and English-speaking, but which is now threatened with serious interruption. Of course we cannot hope that all Canadians will speak both languages. We can, however, set ourselves a high but possible goal and we can move with determination towards it.

I suggest that we should insist that all young people who complete even two years in a high school should be able to read simple French, and to utter in that language at least a few sentences at once correct and comprehensible. In the Scandinavian countries and the Netherlands young people in 'academic' high schools learn *three* modern languages, to which they may add one or two ancient ones. Are we more idle, more stupid, more blind to our duty and our true interest than they are? I do not believe it.

Secondly, I suggest that everyone planning to enter any one of the professions (including teaching), or the civil service, provincial or federal, at any of the higher levels – professional, technical, administrative – should make himself thoroughly competent in French, both written and spoken. It is easy to brush off this responsibility. It is easy to argue that on this predominantly English-speaking continent French-speaking Canadians *must* learn English; and to maintain that if they can talk English to us why should we talk French to them, apart from a few muttered phrases of courtesy.

I am going to tell you why, and I am speaking from experience. I will not ask you to imagine how you would feel towards the other Canadian provinces if Ontario were an English-speaking island yoked to nine French-speaking provinces, and if almost everyone south of the line spoke nothing but French, although this is an effort of imagination that every Ontarian ought to make. Consider instead the position of the French-speaking Canadian who has learned English, who speaks and understands it very well – or possibly not very well, but well

[44]

enough to get by. He is called on, perhaps, to sit on a national committee with Canadians from various parts of the country. Business will almost certainly be done in English. He is under two handicaps. First, although he can express his ideas adequately, he does so probably less rapidly and precisely than his colleagues speaking in their own tongue. He will have the feeling that they are not quite understanding him, or that he is not quite understanding them, or both. And if the debate becomes lively or contentious, he feels his disability keenly. We all know how difficult it is sometimes to make a point in a committee in our own language. We have all had the sense that we have not done ourselves justice. This sense our French-speaking fellow-countryman is likely to have almost all the time. If only he could use his own language to convey this or that subtle shade of meaning! But no one would understand him. He fights, as it were, on the other man's terms. Small wonder if what should be a friendly debate often leaves him with a half-conscious (or perhaps fully conscious) sense of frustration.

Another point, and a very simple but very important one. The man who works with an unfamiliar language tires much more rapidly than the man who speaks his own, as it were, by instinct. The French-speaking Canadian may come to the committee meeting in the morning very bright. He speaks, or appears to speak, fluently, and to understand easily. After a long day's work (and Anglo-Saxons pride themselves on their long days) he will very likely have understood only a part of what went on, and if called on for an opinion he will be strangely at a loss for words. Few people of your years, but almost all of mine, know that extreme fatigue, if it does not remove the power of thought, can leave us almost without words to express our meaning. This paralysis of fatigue can set in very quickly when we use a language (even one well-learned) which is not our own.

[45]

Do these things seem trivial to you? Remember that a democracy is government by talk, by free unfettered communication. When we assume that if a French-speaking Canadian can speak English he always should, we are loading him with fetters while we ourselves are free. You understand, I know, my conclusion. Ours should be a two-way street. When we meet in committee and business for any of our common purposes, if it is English in the morning, it should be French in the afternoon, and vice versa. English-speaking Canadians, if we try it, will find it difficult, frustrating, even humiliating. We will understand what many French-speaking Canadians have experienced many times in many places. We will understand why, although Quebec is truly and completely 'Canada' to us, Ontario may not be as completely 'Canada' to the citizens of Quebec. This understanding should bring a certain sense of humility which will hurt none of us.

I am happy to think that many people are already acting on such words before they are spoken. Great advances have been and are being made in teaching French in our English-speaking schools. But this alone is not enough. This problem is urgent. It is everyone's business. It is most particularly the business of young men and women like you, preparing to enter your professions. You are Canadians; if you have not learned your other language you have not fully entered into your heritage; and you are not equipped to improve and adorn it as you should. Our universities have a very special part to play. I have no doubt that you here at Carleton realize this full well.

To Meet
the Commonwealth

The presidential address given at the opening of the Third Common-
wealth Education Conference, in Ottawa, August 21, 1964. The
members of the conference (some 200 in number) were
appointed by governments in thirty-four
countries of the Commonwealth.

MY FIRST WORDS must be of gratitude for the honour of being asked to preside at the Third Commonwealth Education Conference. As a Canadian, I welcome you to this country, which is proud to be your host for the meeting; as President of the Conference, which is so important for all our countries, I welcome you to this opening session.

Many of you will not have been in this country before. I am glad to know that a number of you will be travelling in Canada when the Conference is over. So that you will better understand what you see, I should like to tell you a little about the background. Here, as elsewhere in the world today, the one certain thing is change. In the course of my own lifetime, I have seen Canada evolve from an agricultural economy to a largely industrial one; from a colony to a sovereign state; from a country with no foreign relations to one represented in over sixty nations.

We have a complicated national pattern. We are a land of many cultures. There is a large French part, a large English part, and a host of smaller ethnic parts. Every part by itself is a minority, separate and distinct. Quebec is the home of French culture in North America and so is more than just one of our ten provinces. Some say that our plural society is a mosaic; others call it a salad. Canada in recent years has received great waves of immigration from Europe, but these new-comers have not been caught up and reshaped – differences are welcomed here. In spite of this increase, you may be struck by the fact that our population is small for so large a country; even that which we have is reduced to some extent by emigration. Though this loss is surpassed by immigration, this does not fully replace the skills and drive of those who leave us.

Canadian life has been influenced to an extent we sometimes hardly realize by the fact that we are a northern country. This is reflected in the way we live and, indeed, in our national character. We lie between two giant neighbours and are flanked by two great oceans opening out to the occidental and oriental world; this results in as many problems as advantages. In Canada there are six time zones across our 4,500 miles of breadth, and we require systems of transportation and communications which would be regarded as unjustified were it not for the fact that national unity demands the east-west links which offset the ever-present pull to the south.

Canada is a monarchy – indeed, she has been one since her beginning, whether the Crown was French or English. Now the Crown of the Kingdom of Canada is Canadian. We are really not a young or shapeless country. We are about to celebrate the hundredth anniversary of our Constitution. That document is today one of the oldest constitutions in the world continuously in force.

Canada has practically no revolutionary background, few national myths or folk-heroes. Her existence has always been too precarious, her dependence upon 'mother countries' always too real, and her peoples' jealousy of their cultural heritages too intense to permit flirtations with adventure. However, as you will be aware during your sojourn here, we are now passing through one of those periods which most countries, and all federations, experience, of constitutional and political strain and readjustment to a new equilibrium. The hereditary sense of tolerance and compromise which has enabled us to carry on over the generations will, I have no doubt, ultimately help us to settle the questions which today beset us. We have learned tolerance in a hard and practical school.

However, compromise in Canadian life has always somewhat blurred our image of ourselves and has often discouraged bold initiatives in nation-building. Through the early years, another handicap was our status as a dependency. But this has not been without its compensations. Having been a colony ourselves, we understand more acutely the feelings of those who travel a road with which we are already familiar. Our only wars have been in self-defence or for the liberation of other peoples. Our tradition has been peaceable, without even internal strife, except enough to make us remember and fear its possibility.

The result of history, geography, and colonization is that there are attitudes and things which are peculiarly Canadian. Canada did not just happen. It was built and is maintained by the concerted efforts of her people. Western and northern Canada have been a workshop, planned and ordered by government and business established in advance of settlement.

Another result of the Canadian experience that may interest other developing nations is our practice of federalism. Although our loose federal constitutional structure, with vast areas of power vested in the provincial governments, has sometimes made it difficult to tackle some national problems, it has allowed the establishment and development of a single state in which the two major European cultures and a host of minorities have coexisted and flourished.

This confederation is one of the two great political experiments with which Canadians have been concerned. The other one to which we have made a significant contribution is the Commonwealth itself, for its pattern of independence, growing from responsible government, was first developed here in Canada a century ago. The peculiar constitutional principles which caught on in the whole Empire, and transformed it, emerged as we solved our own relations with the Mother Country; we became a constitutional laboratory in which the nineteenth-century Empire was created. The new Commonwealth after the Second World War was built on ideas of association which Canadians advocated in opposition to those of imperial federation and a united front which found favour in some quarters in Great Britain and the other Dominions.

In unfeignedly welcoming the new countries to their independence, congratulating them on their achievement, and wishing them every happiness and success for their people, we Canadians also hope to be known as understanding and helpful. Like Canada, the more recent members have been formed by practical compromise through a process of evolution, rather than by the application of logic. Indeed, this process is still being adapted to the Commonwealth's growing number of member countries. Though necessary and unavoidable, the growing-pains of nationhood are always difficult and sometimes severe. They are not unknown to us. One of the great, indefinable bonds of the Commonwealth is the special and active interest assured to new members in facing the difficult problems that are bound to arise in setting up a sovereign state. There are present here today delegations of eight countries which were not represented as independent nations in the Commonwealth at the last Education Conference in January 1962. They are Jamaica, Trinidad and Tobago, Uganda, Malaysia, North Borneo, Kenya, Tanganyika and Zanzibar, and Malawi.

I am one of those who believe in the Commonwealth – I admire its concept and respect its functions; as a Canadian I am proud of it – any of us who have been concerned with its growth could hardly feel otherwise. The Commonwealth began here when three colonies in British North America were federally united in 1867. A few years before, Sir John Macdonald, the principal architect of what became Canada, said:

We are fast ceasing to be a dependency, and are assuming the position of an ally of Great Britain. England will be the centre, surrounded and sustained by an alliance not only of Canada, but Australia, and all her other possessions; and there will be thus formed an immense confederation of freemen, the greatest confederacy of civilized and intelligent men that has ever had an existence on the face of the globe.

From these origins we have all passed through four identifiable stages. First, (for us) from the British North America Act of 1867 to the Statute of Westminster of 1931 – the so-called 'old Commonwealth', about which Sir Wilfrid Laurier observed in 1907: 'The proper basis of the British Empire was that it was to be composed of a galaxy of nations under the British Crown.'

Secondly, from the Statute of Westminster to the independence of India and Pakistan, involving the beginnings of the 'new' Commonwealth with its republican members. Mr. Nehru (so sorely missed by all of us) said in 1950:

We are members of the Commonwealth – that rather strange and odd collection of nations which seems to prosper most in adversity . . . it does teach us many lessons, and in the sense that we get on best together when we meet in complete freedom and comradeship and we know that there is going to be no pressure or compulsion exercised upon us.

Thirdly, from the independence of India to the establishment of Malaysia, the widening of the 'new' Commonwealth.

Fourthly, there remains a period of adjustment in many places. In this last stage, the great decolonizing function of the

Commonwealth is being concluded. Its shape and boundaries have now been more or less defined. There only remains a time of mutation or consolidation.

Realizing what we have to work with, we must decide what we wish to do with it. Now is the moment of our greatest opportunity. To know what we should do, it is worth considering what we are and where we are going.

In the last seventeen years the Commonwealth has grown from five independent countries to nearly twenty. The seventy million people in this group of nations have increased to seven hundred millions – a quarter of the world's population.

Many attempts have been made to define this association of countries. Mr. John Holmes, the head of our Institute of International Affairs, has spoken of it as

> . . . an association among countries of various races and continents which, in spite of wide differences of political practice and international orientation, share, as a result of a common historical experience, certain constitutional and legal attitudes, governmental and business practices and habits of working together. It is a matter of faith and will.

Many adjectives have been applied to the Commonwealth. It has been called 'shapeless, unorganized, unstructured, anomalous, illogical'. Some of our more advanced constitutional theologians have even suggested that we accept the inevitable, dismantle the traditional apparatus, abolish the nomenclature, and suppress the ritual in the hope that the essential faith will survive in hibernation to re-emerge in its own time, transformed and revitalized. Others say that there is no chance of survival at all, that the Commonwealth is fit for nothing but the reminiscences of aging statesmen. An anonymous writer, not very long ago, delivered himself of an utterance rather less than statesmanlike when he said, 'The Commonwealth has really become a gigantic farce.'

Of course, it is not only in Great Britain that some politicians would seek to blame the Commonwealth connection for one or other – or, indeed, all – of their domestic ills. There will always be those who dream of solving their problems by denying their duties and historical or sentimental attachments, to seek the illusory freedom of total irresponsibility, predicated upon no principle higher than a policy of pure self-interest. That is not our way. Because there are implicit, in the concept of the Commonwealth, values of duty and honour and service, no definitions of it can be wholly satisfactory. It has been described as a club, but a club has certain set rules and obligations which the Commonwealth does not possess, at least so far. It is not a power bloc. It is not a diplomatic unit. It is not an economic force. It is not even a group of like-minded people or of like-minded nations. Yet in a sense it can sometimes be those things, although it is none of them. It does confer certain economic advantages on its members. In fact, the Commonwealth is often justified in some countries by the expectation of more favourable economic terms. It has also political advantages. Canada uses it as a counterbalance to the United States. Perhaps for this reason, Canadians may have been guilty of underestimating the economic factor and stressing the political. Certainly the commercial and financial advantages of membership have, for many years, been of rather less importance to Canada than to other members. The Commonwealth has also certain military advantages. A number of recent incidents have shown the readiness of members to help one another, even in the absence of formal treaty commitments.

Besides these non-sentimental realities, we are also a network of personal relationships. A recently published handbook named eighty-five organizations and societies in Britain alone concerned with various aspects of Commonwealth relations, and the list is certainly far from exhaustive. These organizations, ranging from the Commonwealth Collection of Micro-organisms to the Consultative Space Research Committee, reach their apex at the prime-ministerial level. Regular meetings and constant interchanges of information are as valuable as their results are immeasurable. After all, we have in this room today a vivid example of how the Commonwealth can be put to work.

Such relationships and advantages are not in themselves the Commonwealth. They are components but they give us only glimpses of the whole. It remains an almost completely informal association and this, in many ways, is perhaps its greatest merit. Lacking rigidity, it cannot be shattered by a blow in any one place. The commander-in-chief of Hitler's navy reported in September 1940: 'The British Empire is not expected to collapse owing to the peculiar innate force of the political objectives embodied in the Commonwealth of Nations.'

Through its development since the war, the Commonwealth has shown striking adaptability. Indeed, to quote a recent comment, 'one of the most persistent of illusions is that [it] is essentially a conservative and stable institution. In fact, it is a supreme triumph in wild, zestful, fantastic innovation.' Making a virtue of necessity in accordance with its genius, the Commonwealth today glorifies its diversity and freedom from commitment. It possesses what has been called 'invertebrate informality'. It finds its virtue not in unity of policy but in a search for understanding, in the sharing of views, and in constant consultation among its members.

It is often asked what is the value of these functions; has the Commonwealth any future? It is important to remember that it does exist, and that it influences the international relationships of each of its members. Those who have experienced it believe in it, and their attitude must be recognized as partially a matter of faith. The fact that the mystique is difficult to define and unacceptable to some critics does not mean that it can be discarded.

The United Kingdom's negotiations with the Common Market tore the last shred of illusion away from the Commonwealth. It was a moment of truth when the full extent of the post-war revolution had to be recognized and accepted. Many are now realizing that what then seemed a death-rattle was, in fact, a birth-pang of a new stage in our development.

The shape of the Commonwealth and the full contrast of its diverse interests have been borne in upon us. Aware of our differences, and of the realities of our situation, we can see that we none the less form an historic grouping of nations which bridges the many divisions of a much-divided world. The rich and the poor, the east and the west, the tropical and temperate, the developing and the developed – all these are contained in our family grouping. We have on hand a supreme opportunity to help one another and to set an example for other countries in the mending of these differences that threaten our existence.

If the Commonwealth is to meet the challenge of mutual assistance, it must be recognized that each country has a responsibility in leadership. Although to do this we must abandon the idea of the Commonwealth as an English institution, no one will ever forget the greatness of the British legacies. The railways, harbours, and industries that Britain built are far less important than the institutions of government, above all the spiritual values, that she brought to our peoples, and left with them. These have made the deepest impact. Today the greatest testimony to British genius can be seen in the civil service, the judiciary, the armed forces, and even the playing-fields, which stand for the finest in British traditions. It is a record that history is unlikely to ignore. It will be remembered with the contributions of Greece and Rome to world civilization. But the past must not be allowed to dominate the present. As Professor T. H. Silcock, formerly of the University of Malaya, said not long ago:

The Commonwealth is no longer a wheel with only one centre of force and drive. If it is to survive at all, it will be as a lattice of increasing intercommunications and interaction. No monopoly of initiative and concern should be expected of the government, the people or the press of the 'mother country'.

To draw people together is, of course, the function of the United Nations and it has sometimes been said that its existence makes the Commonwealth unnecessary. The answer is that the ties which hold the races and continents in contact are frail and tenuous enough; every reinforcement is worth while, and, among other contemporary international organizations with which it can (and should) be compared, the Commonwealth has shown more internal consistency than any other. As Mr. Nehru pointed out at the time, India did not leave the Commonwealth over the Suez incident because, in his view, it would have been a retrograde step to sever any link that exists between nations.

Though there may be impatience and trespasses upon civil liberties among member states, one can ask how much worse things might be without the Commonwealth influence. In all our countries there is a substantial body of opinion – conscious of the sins we have committed in the name of effective government, of the mixed history of colonial rule, of racial intolerance – which insists that we must not expect all the traditions of Westminster in countries where unity is frail, illiteracy high, and the economy a baffling puzzle. There should be patience and good intention in watching and helping others to solve the paradoxes that beset the final stages of colonialism in various corners of the world. If our multiracial fraternal society has any reason for existence, the most immediate is to resolve these problems.

Our way is to take a pragmatic route to the realization of higher ideals. We cannot all have the same constitutional mechanisms. But, equally, we must not expect too much of the Commonwealth's now respectably established tradition of limitless elasticity. Though all nations must work out their own salvation, there are certain values – civil rights as much as racial equality – that we must preserve at all costs. Up to a point, it may be claimed that variations on the democratic theme to suit local conditions are permissible. It may even be argued that, as regards patently deplorable manifestations, the wisest course is to maintain contact in order to exercise such restraining influence as is possible and to encourage the democratic forces that must ultimately prevail. But there is a line beyond which we cannot go in tolerating the membership of governments that deny the few but fundamental principles that have distinguished the Commonwealth. These are values of individual liberty and human respect, and how fully we are committed to them is, I think, exemplified by the recent declaration of racial equality made at the Prime Ministers' meeting in London. Here we see the unique and constructive leadership which the Commonwealth can exercise in securing the application under difficult circumstances of democratic principles.

Of course, allowances must be made. It has been said that 'people who live differently, think differently'. Countries in diverse stages of development cannot possibly subscribe to identical political ideas, still less to identical practices. There are those who wish to see established one all-encompassing institution, covering the Commonwealth like an umbrella. There are others who feel that structural formality can only assuage, not cure, internal weakness and dissension. Certainly, the idea that disunity among governments can be avoided simply by the creation of international councils is an illusion. At the same time, however, and provided we have a constructive attitude of mind, the innumerable contacts between our member states over many years, which I have mentioned – governmental, professional, cultural, economic, educational and so on – offer an excellent mechanism for a real contribution to the world order. At their recent meeting, the Commonwealth Prime Ministers conceived of a secretariat that I have no doubt will greatly encourage this function. To quote the communiqué:

This secretariat, being recruited from Member countries and financed by their contributions, would be at the service of all Commonwealth Governments and would be a visible symbol of the spirit of co-operation which animates the Commonwealth.

Better than talking about the Commonwealth is the willingness to use it. Here we have a great conference which exists within the pattern of our relationships, a gathering which reflects a common purpose. No better practical link can be found than in the sphere of education. It was H. G. Wells who said, 'Human history becomes more and more a race between education and catastrophe.' If we accept as an initial proposition that, next to peace, the world's greatest need today is a general lift in the standards of living of the poorer nations, then I think it is obvious that broad educational advance should be our primary objective. Education must now be regarded as a human right. As such, it is an end in itself, without reference to costs and returns. Its chief purpose is to develop the human personality so that men may take advantage of their spiritual, intellectual, and material gifts, to preserve and transmit a society's values, and to enable people to understand the world in which they live. Only an educational system based on such sound social purposes can develop human resources effectively. Without it, there can be no continuing economic growth, nor can political power be broadly distributed. Undoubtedly, education may cause social tensions, since it creates new aspirations and new needs besides opening up fresh opportunities and widening horizons for individuals and nations. It can, however, be the force that also relieves tensions and creates understanding not only within a nation but on an international plane as well.

Within the Commonwealth, education has always been a common exchange. Even ten years ago more than 50,000 overseas students were receiving instruction in our various countries; the vast majority of them were from other members of our association of nations. Then, less than six years ago, I am happy to say on Canadian initiative, the Commonwealth Trade and Economic Conference at Montreal decided to institute a scheme of scholarships and fellowships. Subsequently, at Oxford and later at New Delhi these plans for straight academic exchange were amplified to include the provision of teachers and teacher-trainers.

If I may inflict some figures upon you, beside the 250 scholars involved in the Commonwealth Scholarship Programme, there are some 800 students from the developing countries who are studying or training in Canada under Canadian aid programmes, and some 160 Canadian educators are serving abroad in Commonwealth countries. Since 1950 more than 4,500 scholars and others from the developing countries have received training in Canadian institutions under various Canadian scholarship programmes.

Whatever we may think about these programmes, it must be admitted that much remains to be done. There are those who say that if we ordinary Canadians knew more about it, we would be inspired to greater efforts. It is true that as recently as 1962 our contributions to these programmes of development amounted to only some $60 million per annum, less than one per cent of our federal budget. But about a year ago all this underwent a profound change. It now seems probable that in the fiscal year 1964-5, upwards of $230 million will be available for commitment by Canada to grants, development loans, and special credits. Perhaps, as some of our own informed people have said, our attitude is still one of 'How much can we spare?' instead of 'How much can we share?' – but at least it must be admitted that we are today sparing more freely.

Mr. Lewis Perinbam, until recently Secretary-General of the Canadian National Commission for UNESCO, has pointed out that at present the only centre for Commonwealth studies on this continent is to be found at Duke University in North Carolina. He has suggested that, as we approach Canada's centenary, it would be fitting to establish, for the use of all our members, a Commonwealth Study Centre in Canada (fully equipped and staffed to perform functions perhaps too obvious to list), which would be under the aegis of the federal and provincial governments. Perhaps the World's Fair Buildings in Montreal might be used to house this Commonwealth Study Centre.

Of course, Canada's experience is only one example of what is being done about education in the Commonwealth. Every country is involved, and countless people are now familiar with the problems – the urgent question of the supply of textbooks, for example. But for the newly developing countries the need is frequently for people rather than for equipment or money – people with knowledge and experience. We are all in need of more teachers today. Here in Canada we are acutely conscious of this, but our problem is subtly different from that of the less developed countries. We are concerned about automation;

about a new way of life which provides all man's wants with little labour and, it seems, at the touch of a button or under the guidance of a computer. Compare this situation with that of some other lands where the most primitive of methods, requiring much labour and a great amount of time, do not produce enough for one man, let alone his family. The problem abroad is to build from the bottom. We are told that in Asia eight million primary-school teachers will have to be trained by 1980; this would require 500,000 more teacher-trainers. In Africa, over the same period, the need will amount to 700,000 additional primary-school teachers, and, on the educational top level, about 80,000 more members of university staffs.

This Third Commonwealth Education Conference is concerned with the vast difficulties involved and the complicated solutions required. We are presented with a frontier giving us abundant opportunities for thought and action. The great heritage of ideas and knowledge which the Commonwealth countries offer can broaden the framework of our co-operation and enrich each member. Aid for education is not really aid at all – it is a form of partnership. Education is a true meeting-ground for donor and receiver.

In a sense all nations are 'developing' countries. To be economically retarded does not mean to be culturally backward. If many Commonwealth countries are for the moment less advanced than others in economic terms, this cannot dull their great history, rich in cultural and social achievement. We all have something to learn from one another. This is very true of those of us whose origin is European. One recalls the words of Mr. Nehru at the opening of the Second Conference in 1962:

European civilization has a magnificent record and yet many people immersed in [it] . . . had in the past, not so now perhaps, no knowledge of the rest of the world and of the great things the

[63]

rest of the world has done in the past. It is not a good thing for any cultured and civilized man not to know what has happened elsewhere. . . .

Through education, reason and observation can be brought to bear on the everyday problems of man's relations with the world and the people about him. Education opens the door of understanding, and, besides showing the way to prosperity, lets in the light of peace. These, one need hardly say, are goals worthy of our greatest efforts.

The Crown in Canada

*An address delivered at a dinner given by
the Canadian Club of Toronto,
February 8, 1965.*

GENTLEMEN, I am very much touched by the honour that you, the members of this club, are paying me tonight. In the world of Canadian Clubs, yours – may I say 'ours'? – is probably the largest, certainly among the oldest and most important. All these reasons are more than enough to make of this a very proud moment for me. It is made the more moving by the fact that Toronto is my home town and so many of you are my close friends.

Je sais que parmi les auditeurs ce soir il y a un bon nombre de mes compatriotes canadiens-français. J'en suis très heureux. Puis-je, donc, me donner le plaisir de dire un 'bienvenue' spécial dans leur langue maternelle – l'autre langue de notre pays.

I have been associated with the Canadian Club movement in one way or another for many years, and I have spoken in my time to I don't know how many of its clubs in just about every major city across our country. This evening, however, I am fully aware that when one gets to the stage of testimonial dinners one is nearing the end of a public-speaking career. This, then, is something of a swan song. While I am prepared to accept the idea, the thought that this is probably my last shot

[67]

at you makes the occasion doubly important to me, and I mustn't forget Coleridge's warning:

Swans sing before they die – 'twere no bad thing
Did certain persons die before they sing.

I have, at some length I fear, remarked elsewhere that *What's Past Is Prologue*. The difficulty of having written an autobiography, as I have found, is that one can never again talk about the past. The author cannot be sure that he is not repeating himself, or, worse still, repeating himself differently! So I have made a rule against recounting the past and, aware that 'a prophet is not without honour, save in his own country', I cannot talk about the future either.

Deprived of both reminiscence and prophecy, I am left with the present, which is certainly something worth discussing nowadays, and this evening I want to talk to you about a very special part of present-day Canada – the Monarchy. It is your generation of Canadians, not mine, which is in the position to fashion today what the morrow will bring, so my reason for speaking to you about the Monarchy – the highest institution of our society – is that you are the ones with the power and responsibility for determining its future in Canada.

Giving it the earnest thought that the subject requires, I think you will find that there are two ways of looking at the Crown. You can hold it up to the eye and examine it in detail, or you can put it into the context of the community and step back to look at the whole picture. Both approaches have their advantages, and I propose to use both.

First, then, let us consider the Monarchy as a working part of what, for lack of a better term, I will call our 'social apparatus'. Obviously, the Monarchy does not – and, indeed, cannot – exist in isolation from the people it serves. It plays some part, large or small, in everybody's life, and it is influenced by the same conditions of 'modern living' that affect us all.

Speech-makers (myself, I must admit, among them) often dwell on the extent to which things have changed these days. From horse-and-buggy to jet-liner is a good gambit with which to stir the minds of youngsters, but it does not really tell us as much about the present as it does about the past and the future. The striking thing about 'modern living' is not the degree of change but the rate of change.

This acceleration has many advantages. It also demands a price, and that price is uncertainty. Most of us are caught in a sort of treadmill. We have nothing firm left to stand on and so we must keep moving in what we fondly hope is a forward direction.

I am one of those who would like to be remembered as progressive. I am not without some radical views and I have been personally associated, on at least two occasions, with sharply debated departures from long-established public policy. It is not inconsistent with this that I am also interested in preserving certain institutions and customs which, though easily condemned as 'old-fashioned', are still clearly of lasting importance. I find them precious because they offer us something worth while to hold on to in these times of rapid change.

It is now the vogue to consider anything old as suspect. Because great scientific advances have resulted in change, change is often popularly equated with advance. People tend to think that anything new will automatically help to make things all right, or at least a great deal better than they were before.

The fact is that, despite all our material improvement in recent years, it is highly debatable whether or not man is really perfecting himself. In the hurly-burly of comfortable and affluent modernity, many have lost control of their own lives. Old ideals and former convictions have been discarded and have not been replaced. Today, many people – perhaps even the majority – do not know what to believe in.

No doubt you have noted that in virtually every country of the world increasing numbers of people – including many of those relatively well educated – are becoming involved in violence and brutality. Wild demonstrations and riots seem to have become almost a pastime. The ordinary rules of human conduct which have been the source of stability and the basis of peace are no longer in control. There are danger-signals all about us, showing that many of the fundamentals of government and society are no longer understood. If we do not heed these warnings, the infection of unrest will sweep through our bewildered communities and will bring down in ruin much of our vaunted achievements.

We cannot slow the pace of human events, but if we are to be masters of the future, rather than the slaves of fate, we must reduce the uncertainty that plagues our society. We must re-establish the ideals which respect the individual.

Here we should value the role of the Monarchy as the institution best placed to fill this need. Looking at it closely, you will find that it does so in a number of ways. Walter Bagehot lists four in his classic work, and each is a powerful reason for the continuance of monarchy in a modern democratic state.

In the first place, so he points out, there is the Crown at the head of the political system, making it more understandable for ordinary people who take an interest in the doings of their Sovereign.

Then, there is the Crown as the head of the intangible thing we call 'the nation', strengthening the community and its government with the bonds of a personal loyalty much more powerful than respect for a piece of bunting or a constitutional document.

Thirdly, there is the Sovereign as Head of State, keeping certain important institutions free from partisanship and political recriminations.

Finally, as with us today, there is the Queen with her husband and children – the first family of her realms, showing us the essential unit of human society at its best.

In each of these functions, the genius of the Monarchy is that it sets at the head human beings revealing the finest qualities of our tradition. In this sense, the people know they have a friend in their Sovereign and accept her leadership because they can believe in her and understand her example.

How true this can be I leave you to judge. Think back to the life and reign of King George the Sixth. How many of us can say we were unaffected by his passing? A few years ago, his biographer wrote of King George's personal application of the principles of Monarchy:

. . . [he] dedicated himself [to them] with a solemn rectitude and an upright probity. He believed, as did his father, that the Crown must, of necessity, represent all that was most straightforward in the national character, that the Sovereign must set an example to his people of devotion to duty and service to the State, and that, in relation to his ministers, he must closely adhere to – and never abandon – the three inalienable rights of the King in a constitutional monarchy: the right to be consulted, the right to encourage and the right to warn.

So runs this striking passage, and may I add that what is said about the Monarch's power applies to his representatives wherever they may be.

These powers may seem vague and ill-defined, but they are, in fact, all that even the wisest of governors could want. In the art of government, politicians come and go, but the head remains: advising, but in the end always consenting.

The rights of the Monarch are, in essence, indestructible,

[71]

and in practice they provide the quality of give-and-take vital to the working of government. Like shock-absorbers, they reduce jolts to the body politic and, in difficult situations, provide the flexibility which is the secret of success.

The powers of the Monarchy can never be so extensive, or, indeed, so obvious, as to make it a so-called 'powerful' branch of government. Were it so, it would be forever caught up in competition for political authority. This must never be; the Monarchy must be kept free from controversy, standing for precious ideals which are above partisan struggle.

These ideals will be enhanced by a certain amount of pageantry that will make them the more intelligible and the more appealing. For dignity and colour appeal to all men, and a suitable amount of ceremonial has its place. Now and then, when a great ceremony like our state Opening of Parliament is described, revealing as it does the inner meaning of our constitution, the word 'pomp' is used – suggesting mere empty show and display. Pomp is one thing, splendour is another, and pageantry plays a reasonable part in life.

What it can contribute to the stuff of government is well illustrated by a debate in the House of Commons in London after the Queen's accession, on the amount of money to be allotted to the Sovereign. Mr. Attlee (then the head of the socialist party) said this: 'I think that public opinion today likes a certain amount of pageantry. It is a great mistake to make government too dull. That, I think, was the fault of the German Republic after the First World War . . . the trouble was that they let the devil get all the best tunes . . .'

When the future of the fine ceremony of the Changing of the Guard on Parliament Hill in Ottawa was in question last year, it was public opinion, you will remember, that insisted on its continuance.

A party for members of the foreign-language press took place at Government House in Ottawa before I left my post. Most of those present were New Canadians. An appreciative comment appeared in a Ukrainian paper published in Toronto, which concluded with these words: 'Dull and prosaic to the limit, life requires gilt.'

There are those who deny the potency of pageantry even when confronted with such concrete examples. These people profess to 'see through it all', and because they believe themselves unaffected they think everyone else is as unemotional and, indeed, cynical as they wish to be. But the facts are against them; the vast majority of people are intensely moved by a fine ceremony that has a meaning.

And the facts are equally against those who, having no respect for the Crown themselves, believe everyone else to be similarly disposed. Of course, the people's support for it will be influenced by their leaders' respect – or disrespect. Disparagement is catching, and those who would try to make the Crown a cock-shy can do it enormous damage that takes years to repair. The Sovereign can rarely reply except by example, and so the support of the Crown by popular leaders is the more important. Like disparagement, respect is also catching.

This is especially so in the case of the Monarchy, because it is by nature so closely related to our emotions. It has clearly not been scientifically conceived. While, as I have said, its powers and qualities may sometimes seem unreal, in fact they do exist, and it is for the very reason that they are so entirely human that they are real and perform real functions. Let me quote what Walter Lippmann has said:

It is significant, I think, certainly it is at least suggestive, that while nearly all the Western governments have been in deep trouble since the First World War, the Constitutional monarchies of Scandinavia, the Low Countries and the United Kingdom have shown greater capacity to endure, to preserve order with freedom, than the republics of France, Germany, Spain and Italy. In some measure that may be because in a republic the governing power, being wholly secularized, loses much of its prestige; it is stripped, if one prefers, of all the illusions of intrinsic majesty.

I am afraid that I have referred before this to an incident that occurred during the Queen's visit to Canada before her accession. A friend of mine was standing at a street-corner in Toronto waiting for the royal party to pass. He turned to an individual beside him whose attitude towards the ceremony seemed obscure, and asked him, as a matter of interest, 'What do you think about all this – the Monarchy and things like that?' His neighbour looked up at him, obviously surprised and indeed somewhat displeased, and made this remark, 'It works, don't it?'

The question some people ask, not unnaturally, is, 'Does it work in Canada?'

In the days when the majority, or at least a very large number, of Canadians referred to England as 'the Mother Country' and treasured their own personal memories of life in that land, the thinking that supported the Monarchy there was enough to support the Monarchy here also. The drop in immigration from the United Kingdom in recent years, and the passage of time have changed all this. Today, Canadians – including, like everyone else, the sons of people from 'the old country' – rightly demand that things here should have a Canadian meaning.

Some go further. Perhaps as a manifestation of the unrest, of the desire for change for the sake of change, there are some who are inherently against anything and everything that is traditional, and this may even include the Monarchy. They understand the techniques whereby a well-organized minority in a democracy can easily impose its opinions upon an indifferent majority. These views, if unanswered and unopposed, can, depending on the issue, cause serious trouble.

[74]

We hear it said: 'Oh, the Queen is a very fine woman, but she is not *our* Queen. She is the Queen of England.' It is true that she is domiciled in Britain. The Sovereign must have a principal place of residence somewhere, and surely the first and oldest realm has the most natural claim. Founded in the United Kingdom, the Monarchy and Commonwealth spread across the seas not only to Canada but elsewhere – to Australia and New Zealand, for instance, so much farther from London than we. They, too, have a case to be considered.

The problem of physical location is, then, a great deal more complicated than it first appears. It is constantly being eased, however, because modern advances in transportation and communication bring the Queen and members of her family to Canada more often than ever before. Bearing in mind visits that must be made to her other realms and to foreign states, and remembering the fragile mystique of the Crown, which must never be over-exposed, I do not think it can justly be said that the residence of the Monarch abroad works any real hardship on her Canadian subjects.

What is a more understandable complaint is that, by being abroad, the Sovereign is, in some indefinable way, not wholly ours. No doubt this is true – the Queen is ours, but not wholly ours, and therein lies not something less, but something more, for us to cherish. Much has been said of the key role the Commonwealth has to play in reconciling the vast contradictions that so divide the present world. As head of this unique association of independent states, the Monarchy implicitly has a most important function, of which Canadians are justly proud. Within the Commonwealth itself, the Crown is a specially precious link between certain countries which, however far apart geographically, share something it alone can completely express. Tested by numerous crises and twice caught up in devastating world wars, the latent strength of this relationship between the Queen's realms should not be idly dismissed merely because its roots lie in men's emotions.

Here, as on the subject of physical residence, the important thing to remember is that the Crown is a spiritual entity, not only a constitutional term. It has been said that 'You cannot start *de novo* an hereditary monarchy such as ours. It is an organic thing and must be the slow work of time. Therefore, as something which grows, it is likely to have deeper roots and be more enduring than something which is merely put together.' It follows that you cannot put the Crown away in storage until a moment of emergency when you need it desperately. It cannot be hauled out and dusted off at will. It must be an integral part of the people and their history.

In Canada, the roots of monarchy have existed since the earliest times. Canada has always been a monarchy. First, under the French, next, under the English, and now, under our own Queen – for, as a Canadian prime minister pointed out sixty years ago: 'The compact which the King makes with his people when he ascends the Throne is a compact which he makes with us as well as with the people of the Mother Country.' So said Sir Robert Borden. The doctrine of the divisibility of the Crown is the type of mental gymnastic that delights only the constitutional lawyer. All of it that matters to us is that the Queen is, in fact, as she is known to be: the Queen of Canada. This is not a romantic fiction but a constitutional truth. A host of usages underline Her Majesty's place in a singularly Canadian institution of monarchy that has claimed and can continue to claim the hearts and allegiance of all Canadians.

To be sure, as I have suggested, there are those who cannot or will not understand this fact. Instead of using their intelligence to dispel misunderstanding, they compound error and confuse countryman and foreigner alike by popularizing such misconceptions as these: that the Monarchy is a sort of colonial hang-over; that the Commonwealth is a restriction of our independence. When the authors of such silly remarks bemoan the absence of a definite Canadian heritage, they are really attacking the distinctive identity we do possess. If we are told, as we sometimes are, that sovereignty should be transferred to the Canadian people, such counsel makes little sense. Full sovereignty is ours already, embodied in the Crown – our Crown.

Ours is the only monarchy in the Americas. Moreover, it is something that many coming to Canada from Europe know and understand from experience in their native lands. It would be well for some of our countrymen to hear – as I often heard while Governor-General – the surprise of New Canadians at the apparent apathy of some native sons towards the institution. Also, like very few other things, it lays claim equally to the affections of French- and English-speaking Canadians, and this is something worth remembering in these times of somewhat discordant dialogue between the two founding races. On October 14, 1964, on the day after Her Majesty left Canada, a leading newspaper in Quebec, *L'Action*, had this to say about certain student demonstrations:

Certainly, in a democracy, it is permissible to be against the Queen, or against God Himself, and in favour of sin, but if, among anti-monarchical demonstrations, these students take the trouble to study the history of their country, they will realize at the same time that for 200 years it is thanks to the Monarchy that they have been able to preserve their culture.

When the royal visit was first announced, there were those who looked on it as inopportune or even provocative. Some French-speaking Canadians feared that it was an attempt to put them in their place, so to speak, and perhaps a few English-speaking Canadians had similar views about the visit. In the event, and this is very important, Her Majesty made it clear

[77]

to both groups that she would not permit herself to be made the instrument of any one faction in its rivalry with the other.

To those who have said that the visit was inopportune, this, I think, is the fitting reply – a visit from the Sovereign to any of her realms can never be inopportune. As we have seen, there were regrettable incidents that marred what we would have wished to be a heart-warming welcome, but monarchy is not a hot-house plant – it is strengthened by the exercise of its strength. In my view, the recent visit of the Queen left the Monarchy stronger in Canada than it has been for years. It also reminded us anew of her deep and dispassionate insight into Canadian life.

If there ever was a better or more compelling time for all of us to apply fresh thinking to our national affairs it is now, in the two years remaining before our country moves into its second century. Of late, it seems to me, we may have begun to take ourselves too seriously. We have actually allowed ourselves to doubt whether our country could survive, but there can be no question of our national survival – the subject itself should not be open to discussion. Canada, under its present constitution, has existed for nearly a hundred years despite far greater difficulties than we face today. Our country has survived because its people, and particularly its leaders, had faith in its destiny. Of the fact of existence there could have been no discussion years ago because it was taken for granted, and this, I suggest, should be true of our attitude today.

On the other hand, we have sometimes not been serious enough. Our future is something that can and should be discussed more earnestly than heretofore. We Canadians do not want merely to exist; we want to forge ahead and build proudly on the foundations that our forefathers left us, doing so in the light of present-day, not antiquated, circumstances. Throughout the long years of depression, hot and cold war, and reconstruction, discussion of the process of national fulfilment was put aside to make way for more immediate problems. During all this time the world about us changed, and we changed too. Today we are a stronger country than ever before, stronger than we would probably have become under normal conditions in so short a period. We must conduct ourselves in an international scene teeming with new states elated with new ideas. Fortune dictates that now we will take the time to discuss what we have delayed discussing, to consider what we have put off considering. Let us not be too bewildered by the magnitude of the changes all around us, or of the changes in ourselves. But, at the same time, let us not be so rigid as to yield to no change at all. As the Queen said at Quebec last October (I give the English translation): 'A dynamic state should not fear to reassess its political philosophy.'

In this speech the Queen did what in our country only a Monarch could do. Winston Churchill once described Her Majesty as a 'gracious, gleaming figure', and her recent presence amongst us left a lasting impression on us all. I am thinking not only of her mastery of the French language and her familiarity with the values and accomplishments of French Canada, but that she caused French- and English-speaking Canadians to be realistic, to look at things as they really were. Her visit did not, of course, create the unrest that racks our country; it may, however, have led us to face the issues more frankly. Her speech showed monarchy at its best, which, though never a party to controversy, is always concerned to secure the promotion of the common weal. As Lord Tweedsmuir said:

. . . [The King's] importance is not so much in what he does as what he is. We are a democracy in which the will of the people prevails by means of their elected representatives. But the King represents the people in a deeper sense – the abiding continuity of the nation behind all the mutations and vicissitudes of parties.

Thus, under our system, the prime minister speaks for the government, the sovereign for the people.

Of course, constitutional monarchy is not the only form of democratic government. The principle alternative is the republic. Every nation must have a head of state. If he is a president he may or may not have executive powers. If he has these, he performs the duties of both president and prime minister – he is the head of a political party and of a ministry, the wielder of vast and time-consuming authority. Some people see more in a president than in a sovereign. I must tell you that, for our country, I can only see less. If we were to have a president without executive powers, I presume it would be his duty to supervise the prime minister. If they were of the same party, then what would be gained? Or, if of different parties, what then would not be lost? How could we keep an elected president free from partisanship? How could he be certain to personify what is best in the national character? By what means could we secure in the office of president the proper representation of the founding races?

To each country, its own unique political system. What we have may not best suit others. Conversely, it is not true that what best suits others must equally suit us. On the contrary, I am convinced that history has given us a system which, in a multiracial nation such as ours, is more wise and workable than that which any theorist could invent. It was the American jurist Oliver Wendell Holmes – himself no mean critic of constitutions – who often said that 'the life of the law is not logic but experience'. This is the secret of our system. It may not appear to be entirely logical, but it has passed the test of experience and for well-nigh a century has generally met, with justice and understanding, the needs of countless individuals and groups of varied race, religion, and language.

The Queen said at Quebec: 'The function of constitutional monarchy is to personify the democratic state.' That function is grand, but not grandiose. It is real and none the less important for being inconspicuous, and none the less vital for being veiled. The Monarchy is essential to us. Without it as a bastion of Canadian nationality, Canadian purpose, and Canadian independence, we could not, in my view, remain a sovereign state. It is to the Crown we can look to encourage the spirit of nationhood and to warn against its neglect. The Sovereign, as has been said in another context, is not 'the keeper of a museum, but the tender of a garden'.

In February 1865 – exactly a century ago – the debates on Confederation were taking place. For the new dominion, Sir John A. Macdonald and his colleagues provided – so far as legislation could ensure it – that Canada should be a monarchy. The passage of a hundred years has woven the image of the Crown deep into the fabric of a distinctly Canadian life. The Crown has meant much to us, and we have respected it. It is a trust that we have been given. I pray that we will pass it on unspoiled to our successors in this land.

Canadians and
Their Commonwealth

The sixty-eighth Romanes Lecture,
delivered at Oxford,
June 1961.

MAY I EXPRESS my deep sense of honour at being invited to address you? The names of those who have preceded your present guest as lecturers on this foundation can only produce in him a feeling of honest humility, and indeed some real apprehension.

George Romanes was born in Canada, but pursued his studies at Cambridge. I have not been able to discover why a Cambridge scholar should have founded a lecturership in Oxford; this must be regarded, however, as a happy example of academic coexistence! Canada could ill afford at this early stage of her development (perhaps not even now) to lose such an intellect, but as compensation for the loss of Romanes to Cambridge we received at about the same time the Regius Professor of History at Oxford. Goldwin Smith is a well-known figure in Canadian history; he is, perhaps, less well known in his own university. He was one of the first to stir Canadians into a ferment of introspection and preoccupation with their future as a people and nation, persisting to the present. He applied stark logic to the problems of the Canada he found a hundred years ago. He was a natural iconoclast. I confess to a special interest in his reference to the office of Governor-General: 'Religious Canada', he observed, 'prays each Sunday that

[he] may govern well, on the understanding that heaven will never be so unconstitutional as to grant her prayer'.

I recall Goldwin Smith on this occasion not for his polemics but for his prophecy. He was convinced that Canadians possessed an incurably colonial mentality, and it was his conviction that they could not survive as an independent people. They would be compelled, he said, by the force of circumstances to end for better or for worse (and he thought for better) as part of a continental United States. Statesmanship being the constructive acceptance of the inevitable, Canadian statesmen, he thought, should not struggle against, but make friends of, destiny, and guide their people to their immense advantage into the great Union to the south. He failed to see that the Canada of his day had the seeds of nationhood within it. Happily there were contemporaries of Goldwin Smith with the gifts of imagination and faith, which in him failed to complement intellect. If Oxford is indeed 'the home of lost causes', she has to thank her Regius Professor of History of that time for his part in creating that reputation. For Goldwin Smith's cause was lost, his prophecy confounded. Canadians *have* survived – as Canadians.

Material evidence of our survival is by now sufficiently familiar. A Canadian speaking to an English audience need no longer – fortunately no longer! – feel impelled to recite his lists of natural resources, his population statistics, his boasts of technical and industrial prowess, ending with his ritual peroration (spoken *fortissimo*): 'So I say to you, Gentlemen, *do not sell Canada short!*' But survival in a material sense is only the beginning of full nationhood. It is what we are doing with our resources by which we must be judged. Our eighteen million people, our gifts of nature, our productivity, our technology, these are largely wasted unless we make with them something

[86]

distinctively Canadian in North America. One of our poets calls Canada

> A something possible,
> A chance . . .

and unless we exploit the possibility, unless we seize the chance, all the fish and the lumber, all the wheat and the oil, the iron ore and the chemicals, will have been ends in themselves, not means to the fulfilment of our nationhood.

What we are making of our 'something possible', our 'chance', it is better for others to say. We are not smugly satisfied that we are making the most of our opportunities — such complacency would itself give the lie to the assertion — but we feel we have laid foundations for further building. Our constitution has served us well. It is not a legacy from the eighteenth century; it is in many ways the most workable constitution in the Americas, one in which there has been a successful marriage between parliamentary government and a federal system — a marriage, it is true, not showing unbroken happiness, but never encountering any serious risk of divorcement.

We have been successful in our manner of adjusting the relations of the varied communities making Canada their home. About one Canadian out of three speaks French as his mother tongue. His is no minority assimilated within a common Canadianism, but a senior partner sharing equally in the joint project of Confederation. Then there are the 'new Canadians', of whom some two millions from Great Britain and from Europe have reached our shores since 1945, distributing themselves in our cities and on our farms along that narrow ribbon of settlement which follows the common border. It would be easy, it is certainly tempting, to lessen the impact of American influence upon these new arrivals by exposing them to the fierce obliterating heat of the melting-pot. This treatment we reject. We try to fit in the new-comers much as they are, as pieces in the Canadian mosaic.

The plural society pays some penalty for its pluralism. Perhaps we are, as a consequence, rather more difficult to govern; perhaps we set out for ourselves areas of inhibition into which the politician walks warily and strays at his peril. (I could give you examples.) But we think it has been worth it. Certainly the tenacious and entirely natural quest of French-speaking Canada for *survivance*, for the preservation of its individuality, has made our country infinitely more interesting, enhancing the quality of government, enriching the arts, often giving colour to everyday life – as when we glance down a bilingual menu to find 'Deep apple pie: *tarte aux pommes profonde*'. Even in Goldwin Smith's day the diversity of Canadian life offered a welcome contrast to other areas of the continent, as he would have discovered soon enough had he ever ventured from his Toronto retreat to explore his chosen land whose prospects he so perversely underrated. We are told how in 1879 the city of Quebec, preparing for the official reception of a new governor-general, commissioned a composer to write a cantata of welcome:

He was told to spare neither means nor effort for this grand occasion. Full of enthusiasm he set about writing the music and assembled nearly 300 musicians. . . . The climax of the cantata, to words by the poet Napoléon Legendre, was a simultaneous rendition of 'God Save the Queen', 'Vive la Canadienne' and 'Comin' Thro' the Rye' – a feat of contrapuntal composition which created a sensation.

Perhaps a more decisive test of national achievement is the emergence of national character. Can one speak of a Canadian character? I remember often when I represented Canada in Washington how American friends – always with the courteous intent so characteristic of them – would say: 'Why should there be a border between our two countries, when there is really no difference between us?' But we *are* different – each country being properly engaged in its own national experiment – and how important such differences are in a world increasingly threatened with a dull sameness!

History provides many differences between us. There are absent from our story two of the great forces shaping the character of so many modern nations, including that of the United States. For, unlike other North American peoples, we have never turned upon our motherlands; nor have we turned upon ourselves. A nation embroiled in revolution or in civil war engages in a fierce emotional experience persisting long after the event. Colour and excitement enter the national tradition. So do hates, and hopes, and heroes. Out of them a sense of national identity is quickly and easily made. There is no doubt of our deficiency in heroes. Just as we have fought no Revolutionary or Civil War, so we have no Washington or Franklin, no Lincoln or Lee on whose exploits to bring up our young. We need yield to no one in the daring of our explorers, nor, I believe, in the quality of our statesmanship, but the attempt by one of our enterprising television producers to elevate the adventurer Pierre Radisson to the eminence of Davy Crockett was rather less than successful!

But the quiet life has its compensations, too. And I would place prominently among them the empirical, workaday approach to national and international problems, which I think may fairly be identified as a characteristic Canadian contribution to the North American achievement. If revolutions breed heroes, they also breed doctrinaires, and that stern sense of self-righteousness which, if it sustains the weak, is not an unmixed blessing for the strong. Reflecting on our history, we do not believe that injuries to societies may be healed in the same fashion and with the same hope of success as a machine is repaired or an appendix removed. If Americans 'fix', and Britons 'cope', Canadians, it has been suggested, 'adapt'. We are gardeners in the field of politics, not engineers. We are freer than some from the delusion that some swift and spectacular stroke may solve problems which can never be solved, only ameliorated.

Speakers have often talked about Canada's role of interpreter between the two great English-speaking nations. Long before we had even commenced seriously to play such a part, Sir Winston Churchill flattered us by calling Canada the linchpin between Great Britain and the United States. A witty Canadian has recently offered a new metaphor: 'Sometimes for us in Canada', he says, 'it seems as though the United States and the United Kingdom were cup and saucer, and Canada the spoon, for we are in and out of both with the greatest freedom and we are given most recognition when we are most a nuisance.'

I have mentioned qualities which are, perhaps, negative. But are they not essential to the effective diplomatist? And here I may say – without, I hope, any suggestion of smugness – that we have built up in recent years a department of government whose officials are serving us well in the relations we now formally maintain with nearly sixty sovereign states. The department resembles, in structure and training, your own Foreign Office; it has proved itself true to its model.

What I regard as our greatest achievement I have kept to the last, for this is my main theme – how we have become, and why we shall remain, the North American member of a Commonwealth of Nations.

The path from colony to nation in our own history is so well travelled and well known that he who treads it does so not as a pioneer but merely as a sightseer. We need not dawdle on our way; but there are still familiar landmarks worth revisiting.

Young as we are, we are the second oldest member of the Commonwealth. It has been Canada's good fortune to be a pathfinder in self-government and self-determination. The process has been one, for the most part, of orderly evolution. Within our boundaries, we have been taught the importance of tolerance by the influence of our own political and social pattern. We Canadians have been obliged to learn tolerance.

Those who, at the beginning of the present century, showed their enthusiasm for what was known as the 'imperial idea' nearly always, in our country, were thinking of relations between Canada and Britain, and sought to devise ways and means for achieving a single and united policy in foreign affairs. There were two main methods by which this goal was sought. No one could have been more high-minded in dealing with this problem than the members of the 'Round Table' group. But too many people refused to make a choice between the two alternatives presented as the Imperial dilemma – federation of the Empire on the one hand or its disintegration on the other. The dilemma was logical, but the Commonwealth has not been built on logic. The other approach to Empire was that followed by General Smuts and Sir Robert Borden. It would have led to a single imperial policy achieved through the voluntary co-operation of autonomous communities. This ideal was more attractive than that of imperial federation at Westminster, and it took longer to die, but it eventually expired because members of the Commonwealth did not, in fact, see eye to eye on even basic questions of foreign policy.

Canadians, in their relations with the British Commonwealth during the years between the wars, were mainly preoccupied with the attempt to achieve dominion status. It gave rise to a long argument. It is possible, and was at one time fashionable in Canada, to portray this as a struggle between 'forces of light', to be found in certain circles in Ottawa, and the 'powers of darkness' residing in Downing Street and Whitehall. To serious students of the subject, this interpretation of the issue has long since been much less history than myth. If the development of dominion status was so very largely a process of niggling argument and the 'everlasting no', this was probably a necessary negation in the imperial dialectic. We found in Canada, as 'an *independent* nation', what the newly *independent* nations of our own day will find (if they have not done so). They will discover that there is a difference, as Lord Balfour wisely pointed out in 1926, between 'status' and 'stature', and that while the first may, in international affairs, be a necessary pre-condition of the second, the second does not necessarily follow from the first.

The attitudes of Canadians towards the Commonwealth today are very different from those prevailing between the wars, and the difference has become more and more evident since 1947, which might be regarded as marking the birth of the multi-racial Commonwealth, when power was transferred to the two new states on the Indian subcontinent. There are a number of reasons for this fresh and, as will be seen, more sympathetic appraisal.

North America for the most part possesses a common language. Communications in all forms from our neighbours reach people living north of the border almost as easily as those on the other side of it. Much has been said of late about the ownership in the United States of so much of our industry, of the control in the same hands of a large proportion of our mineral wealth; but influence from beyond the frontier is less pervasive in the economic field than in that which is concerned with the intangibles. This presents a subtle and persistent problem about which Canadians have become increasingly apprehensive. Was Goldwin Smith going to be proved right after so many years? Was continental union inevitable? Many Canadians, fearful, perhaps unjustly fearful, of the winds that blow from the south, have looked to the Commonwealth association as a countervailing force against an erosion of our sense of national identity. This took the form, on the part of those who had always had an affection for their kinsmen in the British Isles, of an even warmer feeling. But there is a still more interesting development – the sense of strong attachment to the ideals of the Commonwealth association on the part of those Canadians who, during the argument over national status, were suspicious of the imperial connection – ardent Canadian nationalists of the 1930s active on the western prairies, and some of the intellectuals of French Canada.

But Canadians have become attracted by the Commonwealth ideal for reasons more constructive than the desire to escape from the influence of the United States. We have come to regard the Commonwealth as a grouping of friendly nations making widely differing responses to the Cold War, thus cutting across the frozen configuration of international politics. Also, we are nations which are accustomed to consult one another and, in our individual responses, to have regard for the interests of the whole. If the countries in such a group, embracing on the one hand two members of the Atlantic Pact and on the other the chief exponents of Afro-Asian neutralism, might draw still closer in a spirit of mutual concern, here was the beginning of a bridge in a world where nearly all the bridges had been blown. Against a background not only of political conflict but of racial strife, the ideal of a multiracial Commonwealth offers, hopefully, an object lesson in tolerance and understanding between white and non-white peoples. Canadians in all walks of life are attracted by this aspect of the Commonwealth, even if they know (or should know) that in practice the ideal has been sadly tarnished.

[93]

Since the inauguration of the Colombo Plan in 1950, the Commonwealth is proving its worth as an instrument for distributing the wealth of its nations in the form of technical and capital assistance more equitably between the so-called 'developed' and 'developing' communities of the world. The relationship between donor and recipient is often unhappy and always difficult. The Commonwealth relationship, as it appears to us, has done much, and it may do much more, to keep the resulting tension within reasonable bounds.

These new aspects of the Commonwealth association have combined to produce among Canadians an attitude unlike any known before. Resentment, indifference, passive acceptance, perfunctory acknowledgement, have given way to something that is almost a proprietary interest. This is not to be misunderstood. No one, of course, questions Britain's place as the senior partner of the new association. Apart from many obvious reasons, there is much too great an admiration in our country for the way in which the British people and their leaders have gone about their task of what might be called creative abdication. The Commonwealth is changing so rapidly as even to outpace the efforts of the cartographer. Its past history will, for most of us, never lose its appeal; its lustre will not fade. But greater even than the achievement of creating the old British Empire, whether through 'absence of mind' or by design, is the supreme feat of its orderly dissolution in the new Commonwealth, with an absolute minimum of violence and rancour. History records nothing remotely resembling it. The solid diadem of Empire has been quietly replaced by a loosely strung necklace of independent nations. This process of honourable liquidation certainly does not suffer by comparison with the hasty retreats and over-staying of welcomes displayed by other colonial powers.

Canadian opinion, then, reveals no wish to displace others

[94]

as leaders in the Commonwealth nor a desire to intrude, but only a readiness to share in the solution of problems once thought of as entirely colonial in nature, and now worthy of Commonwealth interest. Old inhibitions have disappeared. Canadian governments have now permitted citizens of our country to serve on bodies dealing with colonial or Commonwealth problems: a Canadian was named as a member of the Constitutional Commission for Malaya; another was appointed to the Monckton Commission which reported on the Central African Federation. Still another has recently assumed command of a British division; a Canadian brigade was part of the Commonwealth division in the Korean War (and here may I say that we are told by its officers that this formation, drawn from widely scattered and very diverse countries of the Commonwealth, revealed a striking solidarity of feeling among those who served in it; when men, from whatever continent they may come, choose to spend their leave together, there must be a very real bond between them).

So we, in Canada, share a general sense of concern when one Commonwealth member transgresses what has come to be understood as the unwritten code of the association: as when the domestic policies of a member too flagrantly conflict with what we know to be enduring principles of human rights, whether or not they are written into a constitution; as when two of its members come close to open conflict over a dispute between them; as when we fail to remember the unwritten rule of consultation before commitment, so as not to place other members of the association in a difficult position in matters of foreign policy.

Canadians, then, have come to think of the Commonwealth as their Commonwealth. They do not, of course, claim any special proprietary interest. Still less do they resent interest on the part of other members, whether settler countries or

Afro-Asian members, whether realms or republics. Just as we have come to accept the principle of the 'divisibility of the Crown' for constitutional purposes, so the time has come for understanding what is meant by the 'divisibility of the Commonwealth', for its new and varied political purposes.

We have been dealing with perspectives. What are the prospects? What are the pressing problems of the contemporary Commonwealth, with which Canadians, in keeping with their particular interest, have come to be as deeply concerned as any other member?

There is the persistent problem of reconciling the traditional principle of non-interference by one member in the affairs of another, with something else – with the sense of concern each member ought to feel when the prestige of their common association is threatened and, with it, its character as an exemplar of decent and civilized international behaviour.

The Commonwealth, for the first time, met with this issue last March in a pressing and insistent form, and no evasion was possible. The policy of one member *did* threaten the prestige of our family of nations. The only possible course of action was followed. I know not all are satisfied by the outcome. For our Commonwealth, the loss of the land of Botha and of Smuts has left a sense of sadness. But it is an index of our civility that there has been no gloating, only a feeling of compassion and hope. What happened had to happen. Racial policy is no mere matter of domestic concern. What John Donne said of a man is true of a nation. It is 'involved in Mankinde'.

Another great problem which the Commonwealth must face will arise as new states – many new states – of increasingly diverse backgrounds and traditions are admitted to membership. If I may draw on my personal experience, I have very happy recollections of the meetings which we four High Commissioners – from New Zealand and Australia, from South Africa and Canada – held with the Secretary of State for Dominion Affairs, and two or three others, almost daily during the course of the Second World War. These informal, unrecorded, intimate, one could almost say 'cosy', sessions were proof of the family relationship between Britain and the old Dominions. What will happen to the Commonwealth when its members increase to eighteen, twenty, or even more? How can the family atmosphere be preserved?

I do not pretend to know the answers to these questions, which will tax the imagination and resourcefulness of Commonwealth statesmen for a long time to come. But it is not too early to put our collective intelligence to work to devise solutions as best we can, and I rejoice that among the first to give the problem the benefit of their attention have been newer members of our association. I was much interested in the fruitful suggestions of the Prime Minister of Malaya. I should like to comment, if I may, on one of them. The Tunku expressed his concern that, as he put it, 'unless the principle is accepted of agreement by majority there is a danger that the present loosely knit association may become a farce, degenerating into a coffee-house discussion'.

Now, with the greatest respect, I submit that the concept of 'a coffee-house Commonwealth' (if I may use the expression) is nothing of which we need be fearful, still less ashamed. The coffee-house, at its best, was an admirable institution, as an English poet reminds us:

> To some coffee-house I stray
> For news, the manna of a day. . . .

It was a centre for imparting and acquiring information, for exchanging views, for trading ideas; and all this in an atmosphere of friendliness and freedom. If the meetings of the

[97]

representatives of our Commonwealth – not only of prime ministers but in less exalted gatherings – continue to reflect the qualities of the coffee-house – or, if you like, of the common-room – we shall have, it seems to me, an incomparable agency for intellectual mutual aid. The High Commissioner for Ceylon in London has observed that Commonwealth members 'are perfectly free to argue and to dispute and to hold to their own individual opinions'. Canadians have found this true throughout their long membership and may draw on that experience to support the High Commissioner's view that 'it is the informality of the club atmosphere that makes membership in the Commonwealth both pleasant and so productive of results'.

The real danger, it seems to me, is not that of 'a coffee-house Commonwealth', but the risk that through scepticism, scorn, or suspicion we may allow this priceless setting for the free exchange of opinion to gather dust and cobwebs, and eventually to vanish. That would be a major tragedy. We must not let it happen.

Another problem is raised by the disappearance of the life of learning which Commonwealth leaders used to share. It has even been said, 'Oxford has held the Commonwealth together.' (I apologize for this note of complacency.) But will our solidarity be weakened as, in future, more of our leaders attend, as they will, as they must, their own institutions, receiving instruction in their own languages? This is not so much a development to be regretted as one to be reckoned with. The older members of the Commonwealth can help, as they have helped, by getting the institutions of higher learning in the new nations off to the best possible start. . . .

A major problem is presented by the disappearance, in some cases, from the Commonwealth of the parliamentary institutions which were once a distinguishing feature of all its members. This eclipse may be temporary or permanent. The unifying force of the parliamentary system has been of immeasurable importance. It has provided a common fund of political ideas and, as one was always aware at Commonwealth meetings, it has given its members a common political language. The daring experiment of planting British representative institutions where J. S. Mill, for one, claimed they could not thrive has not been uniformly successful. If the promise has been brilliantly fulfilled in the Lok Sabha (the Indian House of the People), there are other nations where the parliamentary system is but imperfectly understood and indeed just did not work. One would like to think that in communities whose leaders have been trained in the art of parliamentary government it will survive; but, should it not, we must come to accept and may even come to profit by a Commonwealth composed of diverse forms of government, as we have accepted and profited by a Commonwealth composed of diverse peoples.

All the realms and the republics within the bounds of the Commonwealth recognize the Sovereign as their Head; some as a Constitutional Monarch. I have been asked if, during my travels in Canada, I discovered any difference between various communities in their attitude towards the Crown and Great Britain. I have said that the question ought not to be one, but two. As far as the Crown is concerned, all through Canada it commands true respect, inspires profound belief in what it stands for, and arouses warm affection for the person of the Sovereign. That is true of Canadians wherever they live, and here, perhaps, I may say that the new-comers quickly learn to appreciate the meaning of the Monarchy in our national life. On the occasion of royal tours in Canada, touching tributes are always paid to the visitors by members of what are rather inelegantly called 'ethnic groups'.

There are some people in Canada with strong nationalist

[99]

feelings who think that their end could only be achieved through a republican form of government. There are, happily, very few persons with such views, and they are profoundly misguided in labouring under the delusion that as a republic we could remain an independent nation. We could not. The Crown-in-Parliament is the supreme symbol of our nationhood and our greatest defence against absorption into a continental state.

Our feeling for the Monarchy is marked everywhere by warmth and devotion, but our attitude to Great Britain, naturally, differs with the backgrounds of the Canadians concerned, and their knowledge of the people of the United Kingdom. Persons of British ancestry must think differently from those of other origins and who know nothing of life in the British Isles. These cannot share the strong feeling for Great Britain and the deep sentiment with which the thoughts of so many of us are charged; but that does not keep the newer Canadians from having a deep respect for British traditions. Stephen Leacock in writing of them once observed, 'Leave them alone and pretty soon the Ukrainians will think they won the battle of Trafalgar!'

Great Britain is separated from us by an ocean. The Crown is not separated from us at all, because the Crown belongs to us, as it does to the people of England, or Australia, or Nigeria. The words 'Queen of Canada' do not come from the world of romance. The phrase stands for a constitutional reality, and when Her Majesty, in a speech made in Ottawa in 1957, said that she was going to visit the United States as 'Queen of Canada', she expressed a truth profoundly important to us and of deep significance to the Commonwealth of which she is Head.

The benign role of the Crown has been superbly illuminated by the Queen's recent tours in India and Pakistan, where new republics replace the older raj. Not only did the Sovereign visit these states at their invitation, but, through an inspired constitutional paradox, took part in the celebrations of the birthday of republican institutions in India. Vast crowds received her with a tumultuous welcome, often exhibiting, by way of tribute, symbols of the former British rule. What is comparable beyond our Commonwealth?

The Crown gives to government a personal quality that mellows and humanizes it. When convicts are released in Canada, under a royal amnesty, there are often expressions from them of gratitude to the Sovereign. Lawyers would tell them that such an act of clemency is a governmental action, but governments under our system, as we know, act in the name of the Sovereign. Our allegiance is not to a document, nor to the design on a piece of bunting, but to a person.

The ultimate aims of the members of our association are the same as those of most nations: a profound desire for peace, security, and justice. However, by a strange – and we think happy – accident, history has thrown together men of many races and tongues in a grouping of states where the blending of law with liberty is represented by a supreme uniting symbol. The Crown stands for all that is best in us. Its aura transcends even the boundaries of the Commonwealth itself. The world is aware of it. There exists today no human institution whose influence for good surpasses that of the Monarchy we cherish.